HOME ACCESSORIES

with

Style

Step-by-Step
Creative Decorating Ideas

CY DeCOSSE
INCORPORATED

A COWLES MAGAZINES COMPANY

CONTENTS

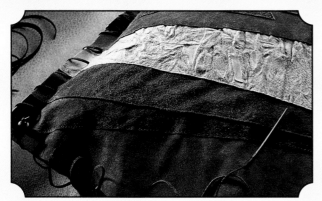

Copyright © 1996
Cy DeCosse Incorporated
5900 Green Oak Drive
Minnetonka, Minnesota 55343
1-800-328-3895
All rights reserved
Printed in U.S.A.

Home Accessories with Style draws pages from the individual titles
of The Home Decorating Institute®. Individual titles are also
available from the publisher and in bookstores and fabric stores.

Library of Congress
Cataloging-in-Publication Data
Home accessories with style: step-
by-step creative decorating ideas
p.   cm.   Includes index.
ISBN 0-86573-397-X (hardcover)
1. House furnishings. 2. Handicraft.
3. Interior decoration.
TT387.A33 1996
745.5--dc20   95-44654

Published in the U.S.A. in 1996
and distributed in the U.S.A. by:
Cy DeCosse Incorporated
5900 Green Oak Drive
Minnetonka, MN 55343

CY DECOSSE INCORPORATED

A COWLES MAGAZINES COMPANY

Chairman/CEO: Bruce Barnet
Chairman Emeritus: Cy DeCosse
President/COO: Nino Tarantino
Executive V.P./Editor-in-Chief: William B. Jones
Created by: The Editors of Cy DeCosse Incorporated
96 97 98 99 / 5 4 3 2 1

HOME ACCESSORIES WITH STYLE

*Accessories are the most personal part
of decorating, often giving a room
its unique character.*

Home accents that have been handcrafted reflect your personality
and allow you to customize items to blend with your decorating
scheme. Create accents with heirloom appeal by learning a new
craft, such as floral arranging, rug hooking, basket weaving, or
Hardanger embroidery. Or personalize accessories simply by
embellishing purchased items, such as baskets, frames, and candles.

Display customized lamps, clocks, frames, and ceramics on tables
and shelves. Easy-to-assemble clock movements allow you to
create a variety of clock styles. Frames can be embellished to
complement your decorating scheme. Clear glass plates become
unique decoupage art plates when backed with decorative papers,
and plain ceramics become personalized accents when embellished
with ceramic paints or mosaic tiles.

Accessorize your table with tapestry or bullion fringe linens.
Make easy double-flange, tie-tab, or haberdashery pillows to
add interest to sofas and chairs.

Baskets, boxes, and trays provide decorative accents as well as
storage space. Make twig baskets, textural rag or leather baskets,
and reed market baskets. Add whimsical painted designs or classic
wood moldings to boxes. Embellish a tray with a tortoiseshell or
gilded finish; or assemble a simple slatted tray, painting or staining
it to match your decorating scheme.

Embellish doors and walls with a variety of floral wreaths and
garlands. Or try a topiary or dried cornucopia centerpiece.

Any of these accessories can give a fresh look to an older home
or add a personal touch to a new one.

Basic
Accessories

MAKING TABLE LAMPS

Make your own table lamps using decorative vases, such as those from ceramic, cut glass, and porcelain. Most vases with a smooth, round top may be converted into a lamp base by drilling a hole in the bottom of the vase. Lamp parts are available at lighting repair stores and hardware stores; follow the simple techniques on pages 10 and 11 for assembly and wiring.

You may drill the hole in the vase yourself or have it drilled for you at a lighting repair or glass supply store. Drilling through ceramic or glass requires a ceramic or diamond drill bit. To help prevent fracturing, place mineral spirits in the well on the bottom of the vase before drilling; this acts as a lubricant and cooling agent. If the bottom of the vase is not recessed, create a well for the mineral spirits, using a glue gun to build up a ridge of hot glue. Keep in mind that there is some risk of fracturing the vase while drilling; for this reason, do not use valuable or irreplaceable pieces.

Select a lamp shade that is in proportion to the vase; often the shade depth is about 2" (5 cm) less than the height of the vase. The lower edge of the lamp shade should be even with the bottom of the harp bracket; select a harp of the correct size for the proper lamp shade placement.

LAMP PARTS

Listed in sequence of assembly:

Plastic cap nut, hex nut, lock washer, and fender washer *secure the end of the lamp pipe under the lamp base.*

Lamp base *is at the bottom of the lamp, with the vase resting on it. So the lamp will sit flat on the table, select a footed lamp base or one with a hole for inserting the electrical cord. Lamp bases are available in a variety of styles, in materials such as brass, wood, and marble.*

Lamp pipe *is inserted through a hole drilled into the bottom of the vase. It supports the lamp parts, and the electrical cord is passed through the hollow pipe.*

Vase cap *covers the top of the vase. Vase caps are available in a variety of finishes and in sizes in ⅛" (3 mm) increments.*

Neck *determines the height of the harp bracket and shade. Brass necks are available in many sizes.*

Harp bracket *separates from the harp proper to allow for the socket assembly.*

Lock washer *is positioned above the harp bracket.*

Socket cap *screws onto the lamp pipe, securing the assembly.*

Socket with insulating sleeve and outer shell *is held in place by the socket cap.*

Harp *positions the shade on the lamp. Metal sleeves lock the harp proper into each end of the harp bracket. Harps are available in several heights to accommodate different shade styles.*

Shade *is supported by the harp. In general, choose a shade that is in proportion to the vase; often the shade depth is about 2" (5 cm) less than the height of the vase. The lower edge of the shade should be even with the bottom of the harp bracket. Adjust the height of the harp as necessary for the proper shade placement.*

Finial *holds the shade in place on the harp and can provide a decorative touch. Finial styles range from simple turned metal to ornate filigree or crystal.*

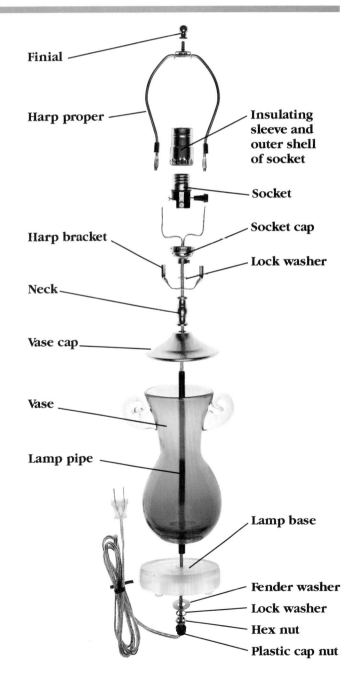

Finial

Harp proper

Insulating sleeve and outer shell of socket

Socket

Harp bracket

Socket cap

Lock washer

Neck

Vase cap

Vase

Lamp pipe

Lamp base

Fender washer

Lock washer

Hex nut

Plastic cap nut

HOW TO MAKE A TABLE LAMP USING A VASE

MATERIALS

- Vase; vase cap to fit top of vase.
- Lamp base; self-adhesive base pad, optional.
- ⅛" IPS lamp pipe; plastic cap nut, hex nut, two lock washers, fender washer.
- Electrical lamp cord with wall plug.
- Socket with 3-way switch, or push-through switch for single-watt bulb.
- Brass neck.

- Harp.
- Lamp shade.
- Finial.
- Drill; ½" (13 mm) ceramic or diamond drill bit; mineral spirits; hot glue gun and glue stick, if necessary.
- Hacksaw, for cutting lamp pipe.
- Screwdriver; utility knife; wire stripper, optional.

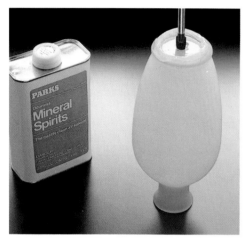

1 Place a small amount of mineral spirits in well of vase bottom; make a well, if necessary, with hot glue. Drill a hole in the center of vase bottom, using a ceramic or diamond drill bit; do not apply excessive pressure when drilling.

2 Secure cap nut, hex nut, lock washer, and fender washer to one end of lamp pipe. To determine length of lamp pipe, assemble lamp above fender washer in following order: lamp base, vase, vase cap, neck, harp bracket, and lock washer. Mark a cutting line on pipe ⅜" (1 cm) above lock washer. Disassemble lamp.

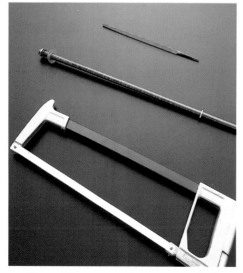

3 Thread hex nut on the pipe, just below cutting line, to act as a cutting guide. Cut pipe at marked line, using a hacksaw. Slowly remove hex nut, straightening any damaged threads. If necessary, file any burrs, using metal file.

4 Reassemble lamp as in step 2. Loosen screw located on the side of the socket cap. Screw socket cap onto lamp pipe; tighten socket cap screw.

5 Insert electrical cord up through lamp pipe, if a footed lamp base is used. For a base with a hole, insert the cord into the hole, then through the lamp pipe.

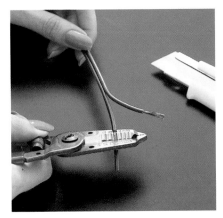

6 Split the end of the cord along the midline of insulation, using utility knife; separate the cord for 2" (5 cm). Remove about ½" to ¾" (1.3 to 2 cm) of insulation from ends, using a wire stripper or knife.

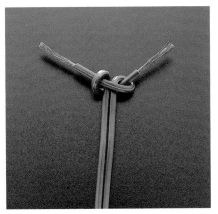

7 Tie an underwriter's knot by forming an overhand loop with one cord and an underhand loop with remaining cord; insert each cord end through the loop of the other cord.

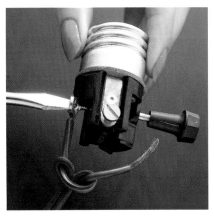

8 Loosen terminal screws on socket. Loop wire on *ribbed side* of cord around silver screw; tighten screw. Loop wire on *rounded side* of cord around gold screw; tighten screw. Make sure all strands of wire are wrapped around screws.

9 Adjust underwriter's knot snug against base of socket; position socket in socket cap. Slide insulating sleeve and outer shell over socket with the terminal screws fully covered and the sleeve slot aligned over the switch.

10 Press socket assembly down into socket cap until socket locks into place. Secure self-adhesive base pad to bottom of lamp base, if necessary.

11 Lift metal sleeves at ends of harp; slide metal sleeves over harp bracket to secure harp. Insert light bulb.

12 Place lamp shade on harp; attach finial.

MORE IDEAS FOR TABLE LAMPS

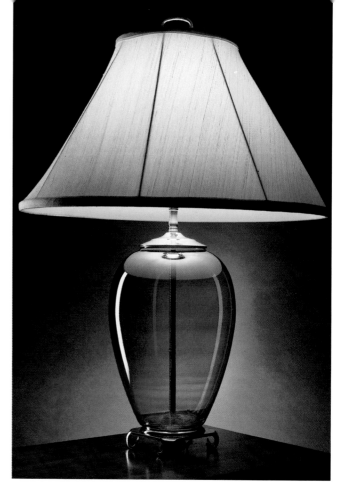

Ginger jar *(above), complemented with a linen shade, creates a traditional-style lamp.*

Sprinkling can *(left) is used instead of a vase for this country-style lamp. The shade has a stenciled border.*

Oriental vase *(below) rests on an ornate wood base. The opaque shade directs the light downward to highlight the grouping of Chinese items.*

Multicolored glass vase (above) is combined with a dark shade for a dramatic effect.

Earthenware vase (right) is supported on a decorative metal base.

Cut-glass vase (below) creates a classic lamp when teamed with a pleated shade. For clear lamps, use a brass lamp pipe with threaded ends.

LAMP SHADES

Make a customized lamp shade to coordinate with the decorating scheme of any room. Choose from either pleated or unpleated styles. Both styles can be made with either wallcovering or fabric. All versions use a purchased smooth lamp shade as a base.

For a pleated wallcovering shade, select a wallcovering or border that easily holds a crease, such as a paper-backed vinyl wallcovering. For an unpleated lamp shade from wallcovering, avoid using a wallcovering that has a striped or plaid pattern.

For a fabric-covered lamp shade, select a mediumweight fabric, such as decorator cotton or damask. Avoid using a fabric with a striped or plaid pattern for the unpleated fabric-covered lamp shade.

HOW TO MAKE A PATTERN FOR AN UNPLEATED LAMP SHADE

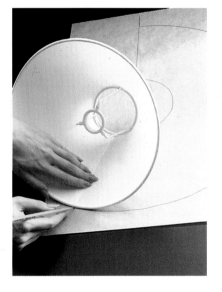

1 Mark a line, longer than the height of the lamp shade, on a large sheet of paper. Position lamp shade on paper, aligning seam of shade to the marked line. Roll lamp shade, and trace upper edge of shade to seam, using pencil; realign lamp shade seam with the marked line. Roll lamp shade, and trace lower edge of shade to seam.

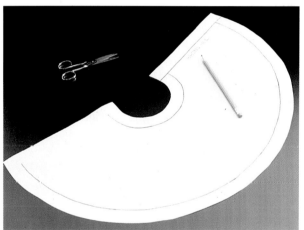

2 Cut out paper pattern, allowing 1" (2.5 cm) excess paper around all edges. Label the pattern for wrong side of shade cover.

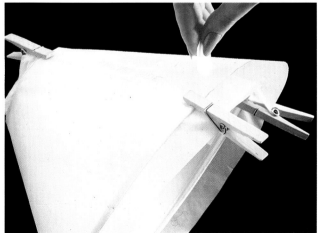

3 Position pattern on lamp shade, wrong side of pattern toward shade, aligning marked line to seam on shade; clamp, using clothespins. Tape ends together. Check fit of pattern, and redraw lines as necessary.

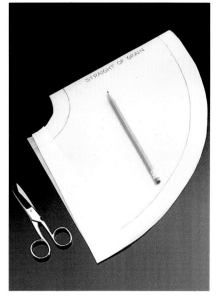

4 Remove the pattern; cut on straight line marked in step 1. Fold the pattern in half; crease. Mark crease for the lengthwise or crosswise direction of the wallcovering or fabric. Trim upper and lower edges of pattern, ⅝" (1.5 cm) from marked lines.

HOW TO MAKE
AN UNPLEATED WALLCOVERING LAMP SHADE

MATERIALS

- Wallcovering.
- Smooth plastic or paper lamp shade, for base.
- Border adhesive; sponge applicator.
- Narrow trim, such as gimp or braid.
- Thick craft glue.
- Clothespins; sponge.

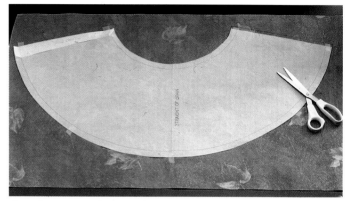

1 Make pattern (page 15). Position the pattern, wrong side down, on right side of wallcovering. Trace around pattern, adding ⅜" (1 cm) at one short end, for overlap. Cut on the lines marked on wallcovering.

2 Apply border adhesive to one-quarter of the lamp shade, starting about 3" (7.5 cm) from seam. Place cover on shade, aligning short end of cover with seam of shade; upper and lower edges will extend ⅝" (1.5 cm) beyond edge of shade. Smooth out any air bubbles or wrinkles in wallcovering.

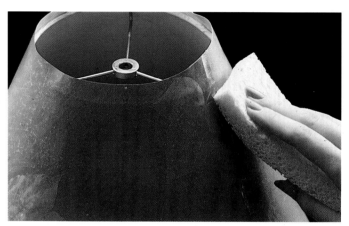

3 Continue to apply wallcovering to remainder of the lamp shade, working with one-quarter section at a time; overlap wallcovering at seam of shade. Remove any excess adhesive, using a damp sponge.

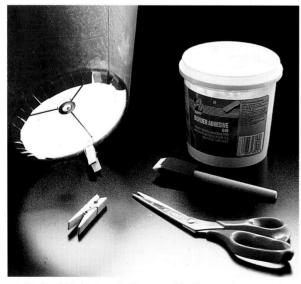

4 Make ½" (1.3 cm) clips, at ½" (1.3 cm) intervals, along upper edge of shade and at wire spokes. Fold wallcovering to inside of shade; secure, using border adhesive. Clamp the wallcovering in place as necessary with clothespins; allow to dry.

5 Make ½" (1.3 cm) clips, at ½" (1.3 cm) intervals, along lower edge of shade. Fold wallcovering to inside; secure with border adhesive, easing in extra fullness. Apply narrow trim to the upper and lower edges, to conceal edges of wallcovering; secure with thick craft glue.

16

HOW TO MAKE AN UNPLEATED FABRIC LAMP SHADE

MATERIALS

- Decorator fabric.
- Smooth plastic, paper, or fabric lamp shade, for base.
- Narrow trim, such as gimp or braid.
- Thick craft glue.
- Sponge applicator.
- Clothespins.

1 Make pattern (page 15). Position the pattern, wrong side down, on right side of the fabric, with center of pattern on the lengthwise or crosswise grain of fabric. Cut fabric, adding 3/8" (1 cm) at one short end for overlap.

2 Pour craft glue into bowl; dilute with water to creamy consistency. Apply the fabric to the shade as in step 2, opposite, using craft glue instead of the border adhesive. Take care not to stretch fabric on the bias.

3 Continue to apply fabric to remainder of shade, applying glue to one-quarter of shade at a time; take care not to stretch fabric on the bias.

4 Seal raw edges at back of shade with diluted craft glue. Complete shade as in steps 4 and 5, opposite, substituting craft glue for the border adhesive.

HOW TO MAKE A PLEATED WALLCOVERING LAMP SHADE

MATERIALS

- Wallcovering or wallcovering border, about ¾" (2 cm) taller than height of lamp shade.
- Smooth plastic or paper lamp shade, for base.
- Thick craft glue or hot glue gun and glue sticks.

- Transparent ruler.
- Soft elastic, about 1" (2.5 cm) wide, optional.
- String; plastic-coated paper clips.

1 Measure height of lamp shade along sloped side; add ¾" (2 cm) to this measurement to determine cut width of the wallcovering. Measure the shade circumference at the lower edge; multiply by 2½ to determine the cut length of the wallcovering. Cut the wallcovering to these measurements.

2 Mark a light pencil line on the wrong side of the wallcovering, parallel to and 1" (2.5 cm) from upper long edge of strip. Repeat at lower edge. Mark pleat lines within marked lines, spaced 1½" (3.8 cm) apart and parallel to the short edges.

3 Fold wallcovering on the pleat lines, creasing sharply. Align adjacent pleat lines, and crease to fold crisp ¾" (2 cm) accordion pleats.

4 Overlap short ends of the pleated wallcovering; trim excess wallcovering. Divide pleated wallcovering and shade into fourths at upper edges; mark, using paper clips.

5 Secure pleated wallcovering into tightly folded bundle, using string; cushion the bundle with narrow strips of wallcovering to prevent marking the wallcovering. Set aside for several hours to set pleats.

6 Overlap the short ends of the pleated wallcovering, and secure, using thick craft glue; allow to dry.

7 Position the pleated wallcovering over the lamp shade, matching marks. Adjust pleats so they are even and extend about ½" (1.3 cm) above shade. Elastic, cut to fit around upper and lower edges of shade, may help to control fullness while position of pleats is adjusted.

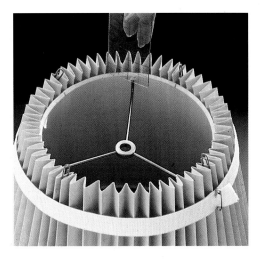

8 Secure pleated wallcovering to lamp shade at upper and lower edges, using thick craft glue or hot glue. Allow to dry.

HOW TO MAKE A PLEATED FABRIC LAMP SHADE

MATERIALS

- Lightweight to mediumweight fabric; amount varies, depending on size of lamp shade.
- Fabric stiffener; sponge applicator.
- Smooth plastic, paper, or fabric lamp shade, for base.
- Soft elastic, about 1" (2.5 cm) wide, optional.
- String; plastic-coated paper clips.
- Thick craft glue, or hot glue gun and glue sticks.

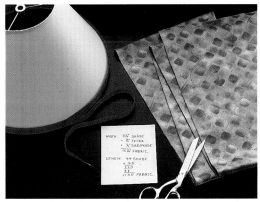

1 Measure lamp shade and cut the fabric as in step 1, opposite; add ¼" (6 mm) to height to allow for fabric shrinkage.

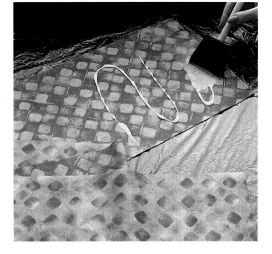

2 Cover work surface with plastic. Place fabric strip wrong side up, over plastic. Apply fabric stiffener to wrong side of fabric, using a sponge applicator; brush the stiffener from center to edges of fabric. Turn fabric right side up on plastic, keeping fabric flat and straight; allow to dry.

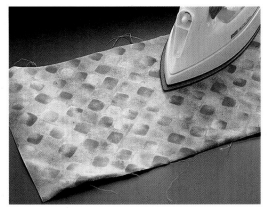

3 Press fabric on right side, using warm, dry iron; allow to cool.

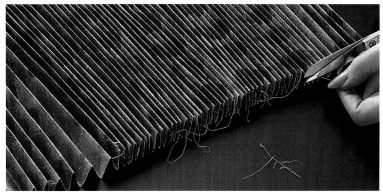

4 Mark and pleat the fabric as in steps 2 and 3, opposite. Trim any threads at edges of fabric. Complete the shade as in steps 4 to 8, opposite.

19

MORE IDEAS FOR LAMP SHADES

Gimp trim (left) is glued to the lower edge of a pleated wallcovering lamp shade.

Braid trim (below) embellishes the lower edge of an unpleated fabric-covered lamp shade.

Wallcovering cutouts are used to embellish the unpleated wallcovering lamp shade at left.

Border edging strip is applied to the upper and lower edges of a pleated wallcovering lamp shade.

Grouped pleats create an interesting effect on a pleated fabric lamp shade. Glue three pleats together and alternate with single pleats for a distinctive look.

Clocks can be made quickly and easily using decorative ceramic plates or picture frames, as on page 25. Or build a mantel-style clock from wood scraps, as on page 26.

Battery-operated clock movements are available in two types: bezel clock inserts and shaft-style movements. Both types are available at craft stores and from mail-order suppliers.

Bezel clock inserts are fully assembled and are simply inserted into a clock case with a round opening; springs hold the insert in place. Available in a variety of sizes and styles, most inserts require a ¾" (2 cm) mounting depth. Clock cases may be purchased, or you can make your own wooden clock case. If you are making your own, the round opening for the clock insert is easily cut into the wood with a jigsaw.

Shaft-style clock movements are inserted from the back of the mounting surface through a small drilled hole; the hands are then attached to the shaft. Several styles of hands, as well as other clock parts (page 24), are available for use with shaft-style clock movements. Purchase shaft-style movements according to the thickness of the mounting surface; shaft sizes can accommodate various mounting depths, up to ¾" (2 cm).

For shaft-style clocks, use a drill bit that is appropriate for the material you are drilling through. Use a brad-point bit when drilling through acrylic and a ceramic bit for drilling through glass. When drilling acrylic and glass, drill slowly to minimize the risk of cracking. For picture-frame clocks, look for frames that will not interfere with the location of the clock mechanism. You may display the frame on a decorative easel.

Decorative plate *becomes a clock by adding a shaft-style clock movement and a numeral ring.*

Picture frame *and a shaft-style movement are used for this clock. Self-adhesive markers add the finishing touch.*

Wooden clock case, *made from wood scraps, and a bezel insert create a contemporary mantel clock.*

CLOCK MOVEMENTS & PARTS

Bezel clock inserts (a) are available in various sizes and styles. A bezel insert may be used with a purchased clock case **(b)** or one that you make yourself.

Shaft-style movements (a) allow you to make clocks from plates, picture frames, and other objects up to ¾" (2 cm) in thickness. Several styles of hands **(b)**, markers **(c)**, dials **(d)**, numeral rings **(e)**, and individual numerals **(f)** are available for use with shaft-style movements.

24

HOW TO MAKE A PLATE OR PICTURE-FRAME CLOCK

MATERIALS

- Picture frame, or ceramic or glass plate.
- Shaft-style clock movement, in appropriate size for thickness of mounting surface.
- Glue gun and glue sticks, if necessary, for drilling glass or ceramic; drill.

- Brad-point drill bit, for drilling acrylic; ceramic drill bit and mineral spirits, for drilling ceramic or glass; bullet-point drill bit, for drilling cardboard frame backing. (Size of bit depends on diameter of threaded portion of clock shaft.)

1 Picture frame. Mount decorative paper or picture in frame. Mark the placement of hole for clock shaft on glass. Remove picture and cardboard. Using hot glue and mineral spirits as for ceramic plate, right, drill hole the diameter of clock shaft through glass; use appropriate drill bit, drilling slowly to minimize risk of breakage. Reassemble frame; drill through remaining layers, as shown.

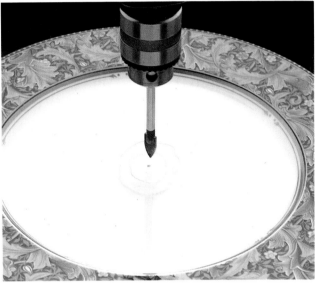

1 Ceramic or glass plate. Mark the placement of hole for clock shaft at center of plate. Pour mineral spirits into the plate. For a plate with a flat surface, create a well by applying ring of hot glue to plate; fill the well with mineral spirits. Drill hole the diameter of clock shaft; use ceramic drill bit, drilling slowly to minimize risk of breakage.

2 Mount hanger, if desired, on clock shaft. Place rubber gasket on back of plate or frame. Insert shaft through hole; secure on front of plate with brass washer and hex nut.

3 Attach hour hand; press lightly, taking care not to bend hand. Attach minute hand. Secure hands with a cap nut; or secure with an open nut, and attach second hand. Affix numeral ring or dial markings and numerals.

HOW TO MAKE A MANTEL CLOCK

MATERIALS

- Scraps of 1 × 2 lumber.
- 1 × 8 board, for clock face.
- 3" to 4" (7.5 to 10 cm) bezel clock insert; compass.
- Wood glue; 1½" (3.8 cm) brads; nail set.
- Acrylic paints or wood stain.
- Aerosol acrylic sealer, optional.
- Decorative handle or ornament, for top of clock.
- Jigsaw, with narrow, fine-tooth blade; clamps.

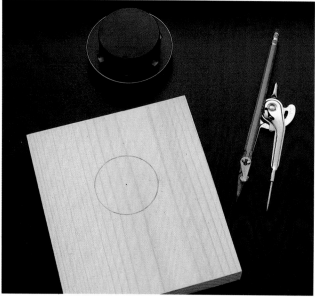

1 Cut one 6" × 7" (15 × 18 cm) wood piece for face of clock from 1 × 8 board; cut with grain of wood along length of piece. Determine placement of clock insert. Mark diameter for back of insert on wood at desired location, using a compass.

2 Cut hole for clock insert just outside marked line, using a jigsaw; this allows ease for inserting clock mechanism. For accurate cutting, use a narrow, fine-tooth jigsaw blade. Check fit of clock insert. Enlarge the hole, if necessary. Set aside clock insert.

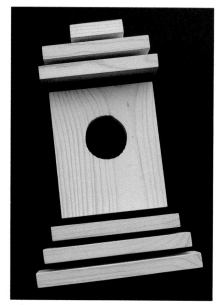

3 Cut 7" (18 cm), 8" (20.5 cm), and 9" (23 cm) lengths from 1 × 2 lumber for the base pieces of clock. Cut 3" (7.5 cm), 6" (15 cm), and 6¾" (17 cm) lengths for top pieces.

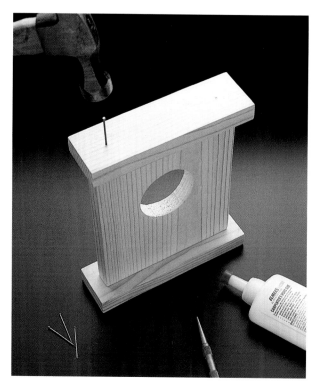

4 Center bottom edge of clock face on top of 7" (18 cm) piece; glue. Secure with 1½" (3.8 cm) brads. Center 6¾" (17 cm) piece on the top edge of clock face; glue. Secure with brads, placing the brads at least 1" (2.5 cm) from ends. Countersink brads, using a nail set.

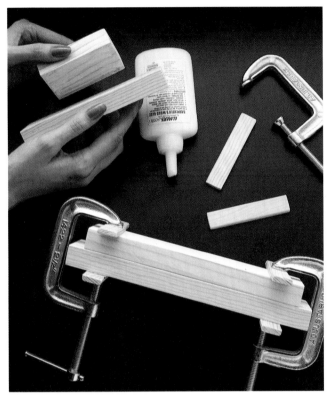

5 Center 8" (20.5 cm) base piece on 9" (23 cm) piece; glue. Clamp and allow to dry. Center 3" (7.5 cm) top piece on 6" (15 cm) piece; glue. Clamp and allow to dry.

6 Glue the base pieces to bottom of clock case. Glue the top pieces to top of clock case.

7 Paint or stain the clock case as desired; paints may be applied using natural sea sponge, as on page 69, steps 8 and 9. Apply aerosol acrylic sealer. Attach handle or ornament to top of clock case.

8 Attach bezel clock insert; rotate the insert to properly align the dial.

Paperweight *is made into a clock with the addition of a mini bezel clock insert. The hole was drilled into the wooden paperweight with a Forstner drill bit.*

Metal frame *displays a shaft-style clock as well as a picture cut from a magazine.*

Wooden box *is turned on its side with the shaft of the clock movement inserted through the bottom of the box. The face of the clock is created from hardware findings.*

Wooden bookend *with a mini bezel clock insert serves a dual purpose.*

Wooden building blocks *are used with a mini bezel clock insert. Wood glue secures the blocks.*

Acrylic picture frame *(right) becomes a unique tabletop clock by combining a shaft-style clock movement with ornate hands and a printed geometric insert.*

DECORATIVE FRAMES

Starting with simple frames for pictures or mirrors, you can create frames that are eye-catching conversation pieces. A mix of several frames in various styles can be grouped together for added impact.

For a rustic, woodland look, make twig frames (top left). Or use your creativity to add moss, stones, or other natural materials (pages 34 and 35).

Embellished frames (far left) are quick and easy to make. Any number of items can be glued to frames, including buttons, coins, gemstones, beads, or charms.

Use a glue that will bond to both the frame and the embellishment. Hot glue is suitable for many items, including plastics, twigs, and bark. When gluing metal items, use a glue suitable for metals, such as a jewelry glue. When applying moss, use a wood glue. Because there must be sufficient bonding surface between the frame and the embellishment, a frame with a flat surface usually works best.

Decoupage frames (near left), embellished with cutouts from gift-wrapping paper, can be made in designs from Victorian to whimsical. Prepare the cutout motifs, following the instructions for art plates on page 66. For a quick decoupage finish, use an aerosol glaze. For a thick gloss on frames, use a glaze formulated for a triple-thick, extra-thick, or deep-gloss finish.

HOW TO MAKE A TWIG FRAME

MATERIALS

- Frame with flat surface in a color that matches the twigs.
- Straight twigs that will fit closely together.
- Hot glue gun and glue sticks; utility scissors.

1 Plan twig placement; cut twigs to the desired lengths. Position twigs on frame, arranging them as necessary for a close fit.

2 Secure twigs to one side of frame, applying the hot glue to the twigs. Glue twigs starting at inner edge of frame and working toward outer edge. Continue securing twigs to complete all sides.

HOW TO MAKE AN EMBELLISHED FRAME

MATERIALS

- Frame.
- Wire cutter.
- Embellishments, such as charms, shells, beads, buttons, and coins.
- Glue, appropriate for securing embellishments.

1 Remove any unnecessary hardware, such as button shanks or charm loops, from embellishments, using a wire cutter.

2 Plan placement of the items; for visual interest, consider using an asymmetrical design or extending some items over edge of frame.

3 Secure items with glue; to avoid excess glue, apply it sparingly to back of charm, making sure to cover all flat surfaces that will be in contact with frame.

HOW TO MAKE A DECOUPAGE FRAME

MATERIALS

- Frame.
- Gift-wrapping paper.
- Decoupage medium.
- Small sponge applicator, optional.
- Scissors with fine, sharp blades and points; curved cuticle scissors, for intricate, curved motifs.
- Spray glaze.

1 Cut out desired motifs from wrapping paper; if using cuticle scissors, cut with curved blades of scissors away from the motif.

2 Plan the placement of the motifs. Apply a thin layer of decoupage medium to back of motif, using sponge applicator or finger; secure to frame, taking care not to tear paper. Wipe any excess decoupage medium from frame.

3 Secure other embellishments, such as faceted stones, taking care not to use excessive amount of decoupage medium; allow to dry overnight.

4 Elevate frame on a piece of scrap wood or a jar. Apply several coats of spray glaze, allowing the glaze to dry between coats.

MORE IDEAS
FOR DECORATIVE FRAMES

Spanish moss and twigs *embellish a mirror with a simple, wide frame.*

Bundled twigs, *tied with raffia, make a woodland frame.*

Buttons and beads *are tied at the corner of a rustic frame. A hole drilled through the frame allows for lacing the items.*

Polished stones are glued to a frame to complement a nature print.

Gift card is cut to make a decorative mat. Use a straightedge and a mat knife to cut an opening for the picture.

FABRIC-COVERED PICTURE FRAMES

Create custom picture frames using fabrics that coordinate with your decorating scheme. Picture frames are an inexpensive way to introduce luxurious fabrics, such as silks, damasks, and tapestries. Embellish the frames, if desired, with trims, charms, or appliqués.

For best results, use firmly woven lightweight to mediumweight fabrics. If you are using a heavier fabric, reduce bulk by covering the frame back and the stand with a lightweight fabric. Lightly pad the frame, if desired, using polyester fleece.

MATERIALS

- Fabric.
- Polyester fleece, optional.
- Heavy cardboard, such as mat board or illustration board; precut mats may be used for the frame front.
- Clear acetate sheet, optional.
- Fabric glue, diluted slightly with water for easier spreading.
- Flat paintbrush or sponge applicator for applying glue.
- Aerosol adhesive intended for fabric use.
- Hot glue gun and glue sticks.

CUTTING DIRECTIONS

Determine the desired size of the frame and the frame opening; the opening should be slightly smaller than the photograph or picture. Mark these dimensions on the cardboard for the frame front. Mark the frame back on the cardboard ½" (1.3 cm) narrower and shorter than the frame front. Make the frame stand, if desired, as on page 38, steps 1 and 2, cutting the pieces for the frame stand with a mat knife and a straightedge. When cutting with a mat knife, it is better to use a few medium-pressure cuts than one heavy cut. Cut a clear acetate sheet, if desired, to the size of the photograph or picture.

HOW TO MAKE A FABRIC PICTURE FRAME

1 Position the frame front on wrong side of fabric; trace around frame and opening, using a pencil or chalk. Cut fabric 1" (2.5 cm) outside marked lines. Position frame back on wrong side of fabric, and trace around it; cut 1" (2.5 cm) outside the marked lines. Trace a second back piece; cut ⅛" (3 mm) inside marked lines.

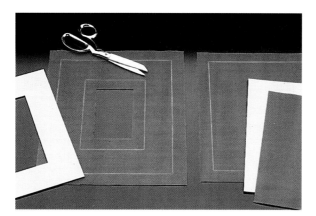

2 Apply fleece, if desired, to frame front, using aerosol adhesive; trim even with edges of cardboard.

3 Center frame front, fleece side down, on wrong side of the fabric for frame front; clip fabric at corners of frame opening to within a scant ⅛" (3 mm) of cardboard. Using diluted fabric glue, secure fabric to cardboard around the opening, gluing alternating sides.

4 Apply glue at one outer corner and along edges to center of adjacent sides. Wrap fabric firmly around edge of frame, pinching fabric together at corner as shown. Repeat for the remaining sides and corners.

5 Fold excess fabric at corners flat; secure with diluted fabric glue.

6 Apply smaller piece of fabric to frame back, using aerosol adhesive. Center frame back, fabric side up, on the wrong side of remaining fabric piece; secure with aerosol adhesive. Wrap and glue sides as for frame front. Seal raw edges of fabric with diluted fabric glue; this is inside of frame back.

(Continued)

7 Apply hot glue to the inside of frame back along three edges; center the frame back on the frame front, and secure. One side of the frame is left open for inserting a photograph or a picture.

8 Make and attach frame stand (below), if desired. Attach embellishments as desired, securing them with glue. Insert photograph or picture and protective clear acetate sheet.

HOW TO MAKE A FRAME STAND

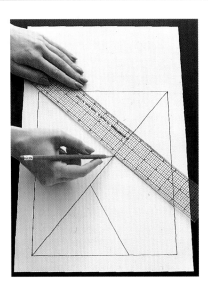

1 Mark the dimensions of frame on paper; divide rectangle in half diagonally. Measuring from the lower corner, mark point on each side of corner a distance equal to about one-third the width of the frame. Align a straightedge with one point and opposite corner; mark line from the point to diagonal marked line. Repeat for remaining point.

2 Cut out the frame stand pattern. Position on cardboard; trace. Cut out frame stand. Lightly score cardboard ½" (1.3 cm) from upper edge, using straightedge and mat knife; do not cut through cardboard. Flip stand over and gently crease cardboard along scored line as shown.

3 Position stand on wrong side of fabric, scored side up; trace. Cut ½" (1.3 cm) outside marked lines. Turn stand over and repeat to cut second piece, cutting ⅛" (3 mm) inside marked lines; this is lining piece.

4 Center stand, scored side up, on wrong side of larger fabric piece. Using diluted glue and brush, apply glue to the edges of fabric, and wrap around the edges of stand, clipping fabric at corners. Secure lining piece, centered, using aerosol adhesive. Seal the raw edges of fabric with diluted fabric glue.

5 Apply hot glue to lining side of frame stand above scored line. Secure the stand to the back of the frame, matching outer edges at the corner of the frame.

MORE IDEAS FOR PICTURE FRAMES

Brass wire is wrapped around the corners of a fabric-covered frame for embellishment. The wire is applied before the back is secured in place.

Wallcovering cutouts embellish an acrylic frame. The wallcovering is applied using border adhesive.

Wallcovering border is used to trim a wooden frame. The border is mitered at the corners.

Trio of frames is hinged by inserting ribbon between the frame fronts and backs. A 1/8" (3 mm) space is allowed between the frames to allow for folding. No frame stands are needed for hinged frames.

MATTING & FRAMING

Create your own mats for prints, photographs, or textile artwork and frame the pieces, using simple techniques. The artwork is matted with either a single or double mat, then mounted on a backing board and framed. With a few basic tools, you can achieve professional results.

Art supply stores and framing shops offer framing supplies. Hardware stores supply and cut single-strength glass, an inexpensive and distortion-free glass suitable for most artwork.

Use a mat cutter for cutting mats with a 45° beveled edge. Mat cutters are available in a variety of styles and prices. For best results, select one that has a retractable blade and is marked with a start-and-stop line. Specific cutting instructions may vary with the type of mat cutter.

To preserve photographs or prints, use mat and backing boards that are acid-free; these boards are coated with a buffer to neutralize the acid in the wood pulp. When framing pieces that are valuable or irreplaceable, purchase museum-quality boards made from 100 percent cotton rag.

Select mat boards in textures and colors that complement and enhance the artwork without distracting from it. Many pieces are attractively framed with a single mat, but you may choose a double mat to add depth to a picture. Usually, the color of the outer mat echoes a dominant color in the picture, while the color of the inner mat accentuates interesting features and leads the eye toward the picture.

The width of the outer mat varies with the size of the print and the desired look; experiment, using strips of paper, to determine the desired width. Avoid using frames and mats of the same width; generally, the outer mat is at least twice the width of the frame. In most cases, all four borders of the mat are of equal width. For traditional prints, the lower border is often cut ¼" to ¾" (6 mm to 2 cm) wider than the other three. Contemporary prints often have unequal borders.

When cutting mats and backing boards, measure the inside mounting space of the frame, and cut the backing and outer mat board ⅛" (3 mm) smaller to allow ease for fitting. If you are ordering a custom frame, the fitting ease will be allowed when the frame is cut; specify the exact size of the backing and outer mat boards.

To prevent a print or photograph from warping, choose a firm backing board in a thickness suitable for the frame. For frames with a shallow mounting space, use a heavyweight ply board. For deeper frames, you can use a board with a foam core to provide a lightweight backing.

Select a frame that is in proportion to the picture, making sure that the frame will support the weight of the glass and has the correct mounting space for the thickness of the mats and backing.

Hinge mounting is the preferred method used by professionals for mounting photographs and prints. It is a quick, easy method that uses tape to secure the picture to the backing board. To preserve a valuable photograph or print, use a special framer's tape to secure the picture. Other tapes, such as transparent tape or masking tape, may lose adhesive quality over time and cause the photograph or print to yellow.

Pictures may also be dry-mounted at a framing shop. This permanent type of mounting is especially recommended for lightweight prints, such as posters, that have a tendency to bubble or ripple.

Textile artwork, such as a lace doily, may be mounted by securing it to a mounting board at several points with small hand stitches. Mat board makes a good mounting board and is available in a variety of colors and textures. When framing textiles, make sure that the glass does not touch the cloth; this may require a frame with a deep mounting space.

- Mat board.
- Double-stick framer's tape, for double mat.
- Framer's tape, for hinge mount.
- Mounting board, for mounting textile artwork.
- Backing board.
- Mat cutter; utility knife; cork-backed metal straightedge.

HOW TO CUT A SINGLE MAT

1 Mark outside dimensions of mat on wrong side of mat board, making sure corners are square. Using utility knife and straightedge, score along marked line; repeat until board is cut through.

2 Mark width of mat borders, measuring from each edge and making two marks on each side. Using a sharp pencil and a straightedge, draw lines connecting marks; extend lines almost to edge of board.

3 Place a scrap of mat board under the area to be cut. Using straightedge, align edge of mat cutter with marked line, placing the start-and-stop line (arrow) of cutter even with lower border line.

4 Push the blade into mat. Cut on marked line in one smooth pass; stop when start-and-stop line (arrow) meets upper border line. Pull blade out of mat. Repeat to cut remaining sides.

HOW TO CUT A DOUBLE MAT

1 Cut outer mat as in steps 1 to 4 for single mat, above. Reposition cutout section from outer mat for support when cutting.

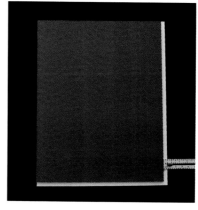

2 Cut outside dimensions of mat board for inner mat ¼" (6 mm) smaller than the outer mat.

3 Place double-stick framer's tape along inside edges of outer mat, on back side. Place inner mat, face down and centered, over back side of outer mat.

4 Mark width of inner mat borders, measuring from the outside edge of outer mat; this will help ensure even edges. Cut inner mat.

HOW TO HINGE-MOUNT A PICTURE

1 Cut the mat board, opposite. Place the picture on a smooth surface, facing up. Cut two strips of framer's tape about 1" (2.5 cm) long; secure one-half the length of each strip at upper edge on back of picture, as shown, positioning the tape near the ends.

2 Place mat board, face up, over the picture, in desired position. Press firmly along upper border of mat to secure tape.

3 Turn mat and picture over; press firmly to secure tape. Secure strip of framer's tape to mat, directly along edge of picture and perpendicular to first strip of tape. Repeat at opposite end.

4 Cut backing board to same size as mat board. Position picture and mat on backing board.

HOW TO MOUNT TEXTILE ARTWORK

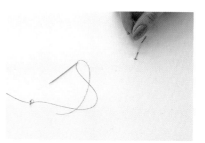

1 Cut mat board (page 92); cut the mounting board about 2" (5 cm) larger than mat board. Center the textile item over mounting board. At several locations where article can be supported with small stitches, use a large needle to mark the mounting board by puncturing it.

2 Remove textile item; puncture holes at needle markings and again ⅛" (3 mm) from each marking, using awl.

3 Reposition textile item. Using thread that matches textile item, secure it to the mounting board at each set of holes, taking about three stitches. From back of board, tie thread tails, and secure them to board with tape.

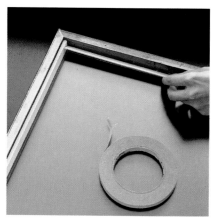

4 Lift mounting board, and check for proper support of textile item; take additional stitches, if necessary. (Contrasting thread was used to show detail.)

5 Cut strips of double-stick framer's tape; secure to back of mat board along inner edges. Position the mat board over mounting board; press along borders to secure.

6 Cut mounting board even with edges of the mat board, using straightedge and utility knife. Tape strips of mat board to sides of frame, to prevent glass from touching textile item when framed.

HOW TO ASSEMBLE A PICTURE & WOODEN FRAME

MATERIALS

- Wooden picture frame.
- ¾" (2 cm) brads, for attaching frame.
- Framer's fitting tool or slip-joint pliers.
- Brown craft paper; double-stick framer's tape.
- Two screw eyes or one sawtooth hanger.
- Self-adhesive felt or foam bumpers.
- Small awl; braided picture wire; masking tape.

1 Mat and mount picture as on pages 42 and 43. Clean both sides of glass thoroughly, using glass cleaner and lint-free cloth. Position the glass over picture and backing board, with edges even; do not slide glass over surface of the mat. Position frame over glass.

2 Slide fingers under backing board, and turn frame over. Insert ¾" (2 cm) brads into middle of each side of frame, using framer's fitting tool **(a).** Or use slip-joint pliers **(b),** protecting outside edge of frame with strip of cardboard.

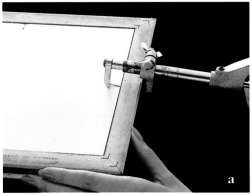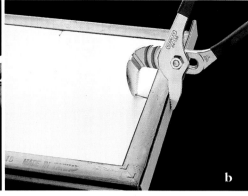

3 Recheck the face of picture for lint or dust; remove brads and clean the glass again, if necessary. Insert brads along each side, 1" (2.5 cm) from corners and at about 2" (5 cm) intervals.

4 Attach double-stick framer's tape to back of frame, about ⅛" (3 mm) from outside edges. Cut brown craft paper 2" (5 cm) larger than frame; place paper on back of frame, securing it to center of each edge of frame and stretching paper taut.

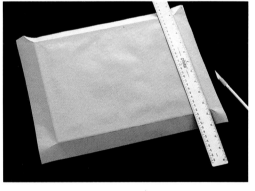

5 Working from the center out to each corner, stretch paper and secure to frame. Crease paper over outside edge of frame. Using a straightedge and utility knife, trim paper about ⅛" (3 mm) inside the creased line.

6 Mark placement for screw eyes, using an awl, about one-third down from upper edge; secure screw eyes into the frame. Thread wire two or three times through one screw eye; twist the end. Repeat at opposite side, allowing slack; wire is usually about 2" to 3" (5 to 7.5 cm) from top of the frame when hung.

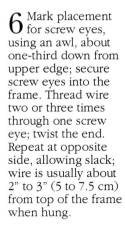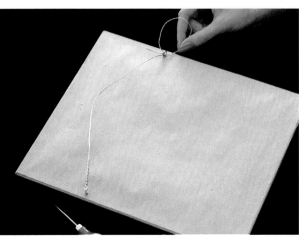

7 Cover ends of wire with masking tape. Secure foam bumpers or self-adhesive felt to back of frame, at lower corners.

IDEAS FOR MATTING & FRAMING PICTURES

Grouping of pictures *rests on a wooden display ledge.*

Ribbon, *folded and applied at the corners of the mat board, enhances a romantic print.*

Prints of Chinese calligraphy *(left) are displayed in large, asymmetrical mats for a contemporary look.*

French matting uses strips of marbleized paper to emphasize the hues of a print. Secure the paper strips with double-stick tape.

Stenciled design adds a flourish to the mat board of this picture.

Metallic chart tape is a simple border for the matted picture at right.

Create one-of-a-kind accessories, such as wall collages, bowls, and vases, from handmade paper. The craft of papermaking requires minimal equipment and supplies.

To make handmade paper, a pulp is prepared in a blender, then poured into a vat. A layer of paper fibers is lifted from the solution in the vat, using a mesh screen and frame called a *mold and deckle*. After draining off the water, *couch* (pronounced "cooch") the paper by inverting it onto a smooth cloth and compressing the fibers.

Many products may be used for making the pulp for handmade paper. For a strong, high-quality paper, use cotton linters; these ready-made sheets of cotton fibers are available at fiber-art stores and through mail-order suppliers. Paper, such as old letters and cards, newspaper, computer paper, construction paper, and grocery bags, may also be used. Avoid recycled paper or paper with a shiny surface. The color of the handmade paper will be determined by the pieces used for the pulp. Experiment with mixing different types of papers for the pulp to create handmade papers in a variety of textures and colors. Fabric dyes that are suitable for use in warm water may also be added to the pulp mixture.

HOW TO MAKE THE MOLD & DECKLE

MATERIALS

- Stretcher bars in four 9" (23 cm) lengths and four 12" (30.5 cm) lengths; or use desired sizes.
- Fiberglass window screening.
- ½" (1.3 cm) hardware cloth.
- Duct tape.
- Polyurethane varnish, optional.
- Staple gun; rustproof staples; wire cutter; wood glue.

1 Assemble two 9" × 12" (23 × 30.5 cm) frames from stretcher bars, making sure corners fit tightly and are squared; secure each joint with wood glue and a staple. If desired, apply one or two coats of polyurethane varnish; allow to dry. Set aside one frame. This frame is the deckle.

2 Cut the hardware cloth to fit the remaining frame, using a wire cutter; secure to frame at center of each side with a staple.

3 Cut window screening 1" (2.5 cm) larger than frame on all four sides; place over hardware cloth, and staple to the frame at center of each side, pulling screening taut.

4 Continue to staple screening to frame, working from center of each side to corners and pulling it taut; place staples at 1" (2.5 cm) intervals.

5 Trim excess screening. Apply the duct tape over staples, wrapping the tape around sides of frame. This frame is the mold.

MATERIALS

- Cotton linters or paper product (page 49), for making pulp.
- Cotton sheeting or nonwoven interfacing, for couching surface.
- Bucket.
- Vat, at least 6" (15 cm) deep.
- Blender.
- Sponge; strainer or colander.

1 Tear cotton linter or paper product into small pieces, about 1" (2.5 cm) square. Place pieces in bucket filled with hot water; allow to soak overnight.

2 Fill vat about half full with warm water. Spread cotton sheeting or nonwoven interfacing on smooth, flat surface for couching. Strain cotton linter pieces, using strainer or colander.

3 Pour about 2 c. (0.47 L) water into blender. Add about 10 to 15 pieces of cotton linter. Blend, using short bursts of speed, until cotton linter becomes pulp; do not overwork blender. Pour pulp into vat.

4 Continue making pulp and adding it to the vat until mixture in vat is a slurry consistency. Stir the mixture well, using hands.

5 Place deckle over screen side of mold. Hold edges firmly on the two short sides, and immerse mold vertically into one end of the vat; tilt mold horizontally, moving it along the bottom of the vat to opposite end. Keeping mold level, lift it out of vat.

6 Shake mold gently from side to side, evenly dispersing fibers; keep mold level. Allow excess water to drain into the vat, holding the mold slightly tilted.

7 Remove deckle, taking care that water does not drip from deckle onto the sheet of pulp.

8 Place mold, pulp side down, on cotton sheeting. Couch to remove excess moisture and compress fibers, using sponge. Remove mold.

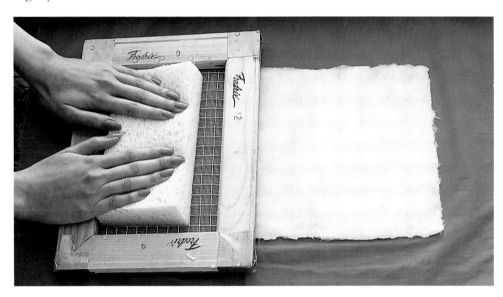

9 Repeat steps 5 to 8 for additional sheets, stirring mixture well each time before dipping frame into vat. Larger sheets may be made by overlapping the edges and compressing seams, using sponge. Add more pulp to the vat after every three or four sheets are made.

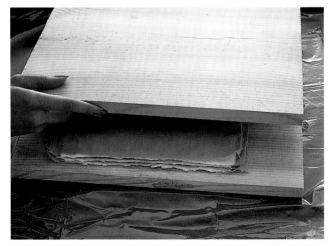

10 Allow paper to dry. For smooth, flat finish, allow it to air dry several hours; then place damp sheets of paper between layers of cotton sheeting. Place paper and cotton sheeting between weighted boards.

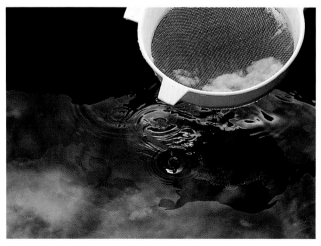

11 Strain excess pulp from vat, using strainer or colander; do not pour pulp down any drain. Squeeze pulp to remove excess water; discard. Or to reuse pulp, allow it to air dry; dried pulp must be resoaked before it is used again.

TECHNIQUES FOR ADDING TEXTURE TO HANDMADE PAPER

Embellishing. Add items such as decorative threads, dried or fresh petals, leaves, and grasses to the vat. Or, apply items to paper after couching, securing them with pulp.

Draping. Manipulate paper while it is damp by lifting and draping it to create folds and creases. Support folds as necessary, using crumpled sheets of plastic wrap or wax paper.

Embossing. Press items such as wire grids, tracing wheels, and kitchen utensils on freshly couched paper.

HOW TO MAKE A PAPER COLLAGE

1 Make several sheets of paper (pages 50 to 51) in various sizes and shapes; paper may be torn into smaller pieces or shaped while damp.

2 Paint paper, if desired, using a light coat of aerosol paint.

4 Mount collage by stitching each piece to mounting board (page 44); start with background piece, working toward top layer. Conceal stitches by stitching in areas where stitches will be overlapped by the next layer.

3 Experiment with layering sheets of paper in different positions until a pleasing arrangement is achieved.

5 Stitch or glue any embellishments, such as hardware cloth, beads, and buttons, to paper. Frame collage (pages 40 to 45), using a shadow-box frame.

HOW TO MAKE A BOWL OR VASE FROM HANDMADE PAPER

1 Apply a thin layer of liquid soap to the inside of bowl or vase. Gather pulp in mold; drain off excess water.

2 Press handfuls of pulp against sides and bottom of bowl; compress pulp, using fingers and knuckles. Use a sponge to remove excess water periodically and to smooth the inner surface. Allow paper to dry; paper will pull away from bowl.

IDEAS FOR HANDMADE PAPER

Woven strips of handmade paper (left), secured to a large background sheet, are used for this framed artwork. Decorative threads are tied to the woven strips of paper.

Wall hanging (below) is created with hardware cloth used as the foundation. Couch the handmade paper onto a piece of hardware cloth. After allowing the paper to partially dry, shape the hardware cloth as desired by bending it. The watercolor effect is achieved by painting the paper with an airbrush.

Framed paper collage (above) in neutral tones is accented with bits of metal.

Bowls and vases (below) in a variety of shapes and sizes are displayed as a grouping. The bowl at right consists of two bowls, with bases glued together; twisted cording adds the finishing touch.

PAINTED CERAMICS

Transform plain glazed ceramics into one-of-a-kind accessories, using ceramic paints. These water-based paints, such as Liquitex® Glossies™ and DEKA®-Gloss, provide a durable, scratch-resistant surface. The painted pieces can be heat-hardened in a low-temperature oven to further improve the paint's durability, adhesion, and water resistance.

The easiest ceramics to paint are glazed ceramics that have low-relief decorative motifs. These are available in a variety of pieces, including plates, pitchers, vases, candlesticks, and bowls.

You may also select plain pieces of glazed ceramic, creating your own design to complement other decorative elements in your home. For design and color inspiration, mimic the designs in wallpaper, fabric, or artwork.

Water-based ceramic paints are available in a variety of colors and may be mixed for custom colors. To become familiar with the paints, test them on a small plate before starting a project. The paints vary in transparency, and some are easier to work with if they are thinned. Ceramic paints often result in an uneven coverage; this becomes part of the unique character of each piece. You may want to spread the paints thinly, allowing the brush marks to show, in order to emphasize the hand-painted quality of the design. When painting raised motifs, thin the paints as necessary to allow the texture of the relief to show.

Use ceramic paints for decorative items only. Although nontoxic, these paints are not recommended for eating or drinking utensils where food will come into contact with the paint. Heat-hardened pieces may be gently washed in cool water with a mild detergent; do not soak the pieces in water. With some paints, the heat-hardened ceramics may be washed in the dishwasher; refer to the manufacturer's label.

MATERIALS

- Water-based ceramic paints.
- Artist's brushes, such as a liner for small areas and a flat shader for larger areas.
- Pallette, such as a plastic lid.
- Fine-point marking pen, tracing paper, graphite paper, and Con-Tact® self-adhesive vinyl, for marking original designs.

Ceramic accessories *may be painted with original designs (above). Or the raised motifs on sculptured ceramics (opposite) may be painted to emphasize the detailing.*

57

HOW TO PAINT RAISED-MOTIF CERAMICS

1 Test the consistency of the paint on bottom of item to be painted or on a separate ceramic item. Paint dominant motifs. If desired, mix two or three shades of paint, distributing shades evenly among motifs. Allow to dry.

2 Paint secondary motifs, such as leaves, working with mixed shades of a color, if desired. Allow to dry.

3 Paint any small, detailed areas, such as tendrils or berries, thinning the paint, if necessary, to allow the raised design to show through. Allow to dry.

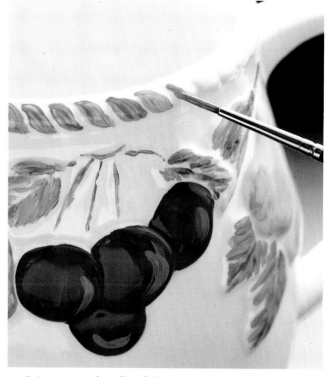

4 Paint rims or handle, if desired. Allow to dry. Bake finished piece in low-temperature oven, following manufacturer's directions.

HOW TO PAINT ORIGINAL DESIGNS ON CERAMICS

1 Trace design motifs onto tissue paper, and transfer design to ceramic, using carbon or graphite paper **(a).** Or draw designs directly on ceramics, using fine-point marking pen **(b).**

2 Apply self-adhesive vinyl to ceramic item to mask off areas that are to remain white, such as the center area of a plate; this helps in painting smooth, even edges. Use a mat knife to trim vinyl edges.

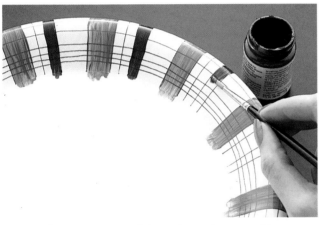

3 Test the consistency of the paint on bottom of item to be painted or on a separate ceramic item. Paint the design areas, one color at a time, allowing the paint to dry before proceeding to the next color; the paint may overlap the vinyl in masked areas.

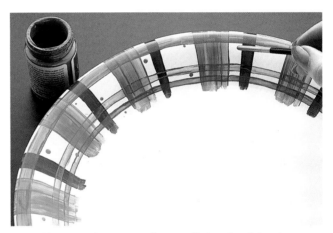

4 Add any outlining or other small details of the design over previous paint.

5 Remove the self-adhesive vinyl after paint has dried. Bake finished piece in low-temperature oven, following manufacturer's directions.

MOSAIC
ACCESSORIES

The art of mosaic transforms a utilitarian vase into a dramatic piece of artwork. Made from broken or cut tiles separated by sanded grout, each mosaic piece has a unique quality. Tiles can be applied over any surface that is clean, dry, and structurally sound. If the surface is glossy, lightly sand it before applying the tiles.

Ceramic tiles, available in matte and gloss finishes, may be cut into squares or rectangles no smaller than ¾" (2 cm), or into random shapes, then applied to a vase, clay pot, or other accessory. Large tiles are sold individually, and smaller tiles may be purchased in sheets that cover about 1 sq. ft. (30.5 sq. cm); tiles in sheets may be pulled off the mesh backing.

The ceramic tiles are cut into the desired shapes and sizes with a tile cutter. The surface of the tile is first scored with the tool's cutting wheel. Then the tile is broken along the scored line by pressing the breaking wings of the cutter against the tile.

Several types of tile cutters are available. A hand cutter may be used for cutting the softer tiles. With this cutter, you will need to measure the cutting lines and mark them on the tile with a marking pen; the markings can be wiped off with a dampened rag after the tile is cut.

For tiles that are so hard they cannot be cut successfully with a hand cutter, use a large commercial-type cutter, which may be borrowed or rented from a tile store. The commercial-type cutter is more convenient for cutting tiles into exact dimensions without having to mark the cutting lines. Set the guide on the cutter for the desired dimension; then lay the tile on the cutter against the guide. You will still need a hand cutter to break the tiles, because the breaking wings on a commercial-type cutter are too wide to break the small pieces necessary for making mosaic designs.

To cut random-shaped pieces of tile, use the breaking wings of a hand cutter without scoring the tile. Grip the tile against the breaking wings, and squeeze firmly. When using a hand cutter, you may want to break the tiles inside a paper bag, as a safety precaution and to help keep the work area clean.

Plan the mosaic design before beginning. Measure the space on the vase or pot to determine the size of the tiles to be cut. If you want to work in rows, determine the number of rows that will fit, planning to space the tiles ⅛" to ¼" (3 to 6 mm) apart. Keep in mind that the spacing between the tiles does not have to be exact; some irregularity adds to the unique character of the piece.

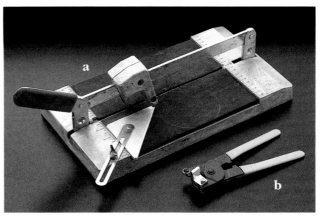

Tile cutters include a commercial-type cutter **(a)** for cutting hard tiles and a hand cutter **(b)** for cutting softer tiles.

MATERIALS

- Vase, clay pot, or other accessory.
- Ceramic tiles in matte or gloss finish; shards of pottery may be substituted.
- Ceramic adhesive or multipurpose household adhesive, such as Liquid Nails®.
- Tile cutter.
- Sanded tile grout and grout float.
- Plastic ice-cream bucket; rubber gloves.
- Cellulose sponge.
- Coarse nylon sponge.
- Self-adhesive felt pad, for bottom of vase or pot.
- Grout sealer, optional.

HOW TO MAKE A MOSAIC VASE

1 Set the guide on commercial-type tile cutter to desired width. If using a hand cutter, mark cutting line on tile. Score tile with cutting wheel by pulling wheel firmly and slowly across tile.

2 Break tile along the scored line with a hand cutter, centering scored line between breaking wings. Press with slow, steady motion.

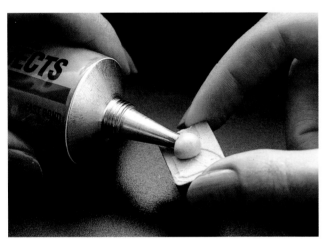

3 Squeeze a pea-size bead of adhesive onto the wrong side of the tile.

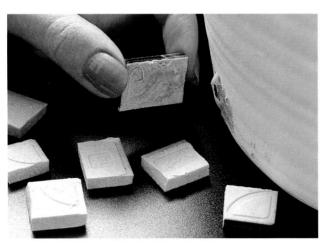

4 Press the tile onto the clay vase or pot in the desired location, beginning with narrowest portion of vase or pot. For faster setting, pull tile away from vase; air dry for 5 to 8 minutes.

5 Continue applying tiles as in step 4. Allow adhesive to cure for 16 to 24 hours, until the tiles have firmly set.

6 Prepare the sanded grout according to the manufacturer's directions.

7 Apply grout by drawing grout float across tiles at a slight angle to the surface, forcing the grout into spaces between tiles; wear rubber gloves. Use the short side of the grout float for small projects, the longer side for large projects. Go over each area two or three times, making sure grout is worked in thoroughly, filling in all gaps and air holes.

8 Remove the excess grout from tiles, using a dampened cellulose sponge, after about 20 minutes or when grout is firm, but not completely hardened; rub dampened sponge in circular motion over tiles.

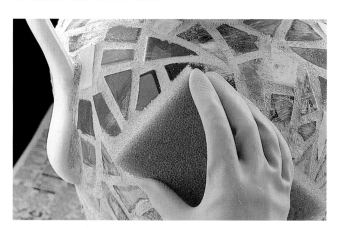

9 Rub the tiles with a coarse nylon sponge to remove the haze, 2 or 3 hours after the first cleaning was done with dampened cellulose sponge.

10 Paint inside of vase, or any areas not covered with mosaic, with grout that has been diluted with water to a thin consistency. Polish the tiles with a clean, dry cloth. Apply grout sealer, if desired.

Mosaic tabletop *transforms this small table into a unique accent piece. Apply the tiles to an existing tabletop or to a top cut from plywood.*

64

Plaster pedestal is decorated with tiles. The scrollwork areas of the pedestal are painted with sanded grout that has been thinned with water.

Shallow bowl is created by covering a terra-cotta saucer with mosaic tiles inside and out.

Shards of pottery have been substituted for tiles, for a more irregular piece of artwork.

DECOUPAGE ART PLATES

Transform a clear glass plate into a unique decorative plate, using simple decoupage techniques and motifs cut from gift-wrapping paper. The motifs are glued to the back of the plate with a decoupage medium. For a background with a dimensional effect, paints are then applied, using a sponging technique. Varnish is applied as a sealer over the sponged paint.

For the motifs, select high-quality gift-wrapping papers, often sold in individual sheets; avoid papers that are very light in weight. Designs from greeting cards and antique reproduction prints may also be used for motifs. For best results when working with heavy papers such as greeting cards, reduce the thickness by peeling away one or more layers.

MATERIALS

- Clear glass plate.
- Gift-wrapping paper.
- Decoupage medium; brush or sponge applicator.
- Acrylic paints; small piece of natural sea sponge, for applying paints.
- Scissors with fine, sharp blades and points.
- Curved cuticle scissors, for intricate, curved motifs.
- Aerosol acrylic sealer.
- Sponge or brayer.

HOW TO MAKE A DECOUPAGE ART PLATE

1 Cut out the desired motifs from gift-wrapping paper; if using cuticle scissors, cut with curved blades away from motif.

2 Outline paper motifs or highlight the designs, using marking pens, if desired. Seal the ink with aerosol acrylic sealer.

3 Trace the plate on piece of paper; plan placement of motifs. Clean the back of plate thoroughly, using glass cleaner and lint-free rag; place plate face down on table.

4 Apply a thin layer of decoupage medium to the front of center foreground motif, using sponge applicator or finger.

5 Position the motif on back of plate; smooth out bubbles or wrinkles, using a dampened sponge or brayer. Any excess decoupage medium around edges of the motif will not show when the plate is painted.

6 Continue applying motifs, working out from center of plate; if motifs are layered, work from foreground to background. Allow decoupage medium to dry.

7 Apply thin coat of decoupage medium to the back of the motifs as a sealer; allow to dry.

8 Apply the lightest color of acrylic paint, using natural sea sponge; apply sparingly.

9 Apply remaining layers of paint, finishing with darkest color. If desired, paint back of plate a solid color, using an aerosol acrylic paint.

10 Personalize plate with signature and date, using permanent-ink marking pen.

11 Apply light coat of aerosol acrylic sealer; allow sealer to dry. Apply second coat.

DECORATING
WITH CANDLES

Because candlelight gives such a warm glow to the dinner table, it should not be reserved only for important occasions. Candles add atmosphere, making any dinner party more intimate and cozy.

The type of candles you select depends on the mood you want to create. For an elegant look, use tall, graceful tapers, or create a homier look with votive candles and pillars.

Metal accents *embellish the candle holders opposite. The punched-copper votive candle holder (page 72) features ornamental buttons or charms at the corners. Candlelight shines through the holes in the copper. Ornamental charms or buttons can also be attached to the sides of candlesticks, using a hot glue gun.*

Votive candles with glass stones *(right) have a simple, yet elegant, look. The stones are available in many colors, to complement any table setting.*

Woodland votive candles *(below), grouped for greater effect, enhance a country decorating scheme. Some are surrounded by grapevine, some covered with moss, and some wrapped with galax leaves.*

HOW TO MAKE A PUNCHED-COPPER
VOTIVE OR CHIMNEY CANDLE

MATERIALS

- Square or round votive or chimney candle.
- Copper sheets, available at craft stores.
- Ornamental charms or buttons.
- ¼" (6 mm) graph paper; graphite paper.
- Plywood; tin snips or utility scissors.
- Fine brass wire, such as 28-gauge.
- Rubber mallet; punch tool or awl.
- 100-grit sandpaper; 0000 steel wool.
- Aerosol clear acrylic sealer.

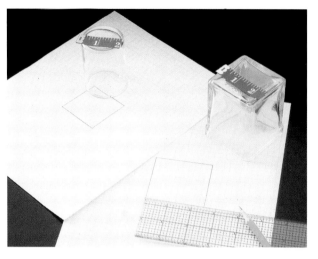

1 Measure across the base of square or round votive cup or chimney. On graph paper, draw a square, centered on the grid, to this base measurement or up to ¼" (6 mm) larger.

2 Extend each line of square an amount equal to desired height of copper sides. Connect ends of lines on each side, to complete pattern.

3 Place a piece of plywood on several layers of newspaper, to protect the tabletop. Tape copper sheet to plywood; place graphite paper, then the pattern, over the copper. Tape the pattern in place. Trace along the outer edges of the pattern, using a pencil; this makes graphite lines on copper.

4 Remove the graphite paper, leaving pattern and copper sheet in same position. Punch the copper at the desired intersections of grid on extended sides, hitting the punch tool firmly with a rubber mallet. Do not punch the center square of pattern.

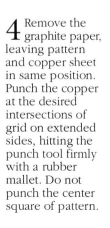

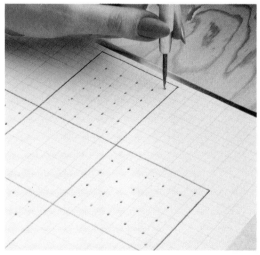

5 Punch holes ¼" (6 mm) from outer corners on each side.

72

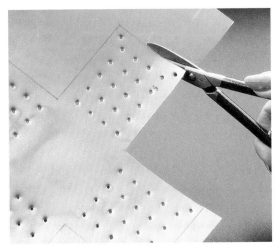

6 Remove pattern. Cut copper on outer lines, using utility scissors or tin snips.

7 Trim across the corners diagonally for a scant ⅛" (3 mm). Sand edges of copper, using 100-grit sandpaper. Buff surface of copper, using 0000 steel wool.

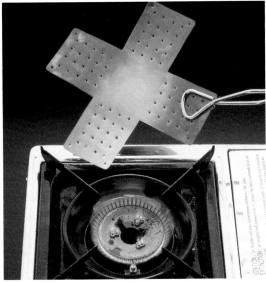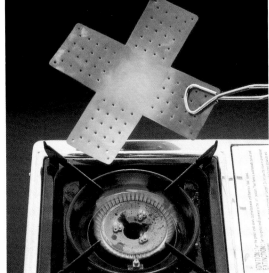

8 Oxidize copper, if desired, by holding it over a flame, using rubber-handled tongs to protect hands from the hot metal.

9 Apply several light coats of aerosol clear acrylic sealer to both sides of copper. Fold sides up, using straightedge.

11 Secure ornamental buttons or charms with wire, and curl ends of wire over a pencil as desired.

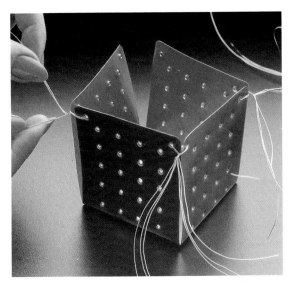

10 Thread several 10" (25.5 cm) lengths of brass wire through corner holes of adjacent sides; twist wire, to tie sides together.

HOW TO MAKE A VOTIVE OR CHIMNEY CANDLE
WITH GLASS STONES

MATERIALS

- Glass stones.
- Square or round votive or chimney candle.
- Hot glue gun and glue sticks.

1 Secure a row of glass stones around bottom of votive cup or chimney.

2 Continue to add glass stones to entire votive cup or chimney, staggering stones from row to row; allow rows to be somewhat irregular.

HOW TO MAKE A VOTIVE CANDLE WITH GRAPEVINE

MATERIALS

- Three grapevine wreaths with 2" (5 cm) centers.
- Round votive candle.
- Embellishments, if desired.
- Hot glue gun and glue sticks, to secure embellishments.

1 Slide grapevine wreaths over votive cup, one at a time.

2 Embellish with dried naturals, if desired, securing them with hot glue.

HOW TO MAKE A VOTIVE CANDLE
WITH MOSS OR GALAX LEAVES

MATERIALS

- Square or round votive candle.
- Sheet moss and embellishments, such as seed pods, twigs, and bittersweet, for moss-covered candle.
- Small, fresh galax leaves, available from a floral shop, and raffia, for leaf-covered candle.
- Craft glue; hot glue gun and glue sticks.

1 **Moss-covered candle.** Tear sheet moss to size, so it will cover the votive cup.

2 Apply thin layer of craft glue to one area or side of votive cup. Press the sheet moss over the glue until set; the glue will be clear when it is completely dry.

3 Continue to secure moss with craft glue until votive cup is covered. Allow for some open areas in moss, so candlelight will shine through the glass.

4 Embellish with dried naturals, if desired, gluing them to moss.

Leaf-covered candle. Wrap galax leaves around votive cup, overlapping them as desired; secure leaves as necessary with a small amount of hot glue. Avoid extending leaves above votive cup. Tie raffia around votive cup.

The warm glow of candles makes a room inviting. A wide array of candles is available, from slender tapers to chunky pillars.

For a romantic touch, use delicate French ribbon to add bows and streamers to candles. Or secure embellishments to a chimney-style candle with floral adhesive or rubber bands, which are then concealed with ribbon or raffia.

Candles can be quickly embellished with decorative nail heads. To avoid excessive cracking, use nail heads with prongs not longer than ⅛" (3 mm) and press the prongs gently into the candle.

Clusters of candles create a simple centerpiece with impact. Opposite, the pillar candles are enhanced with French ribbons and studded with decorative nail heads.

Chimney-style candles can be surrounded by sprigs of holly and evergreen. Or twigs can be tied around the chimney with raffia.

Floating candles and smooth glass stones in a clear, heavy dish suggest the tranquility of a woodland pool.

77

JAR-IN-A-JAR
CANDLES

Recycle jars to make decorative containers for votive candles. A small jar containing the votive candle is placed inside a larger jar, and the space between them is filled with embellishments. When lit, the candle softly illuminates the embellishments.

A variety of looks can be achieved, using marbles, pods, leaves, dried flowers, colored pasta, potpourri, and shells. For a woodland look, wrap the inner jar with dried naturals, such as lavender, and place it on a piece of floral foam that has been covered with moss.

When filling the space between the jars with dense items, use an inner jar that is only slightly smaller than the outer jar and do not place the items too closely together. If the space between the jars is too wide or too solidly filled, the light from the candle will not glow through the embellishments.

MATERIALS

- Jars.
- Votive candle.
- Floral adhesive.
- Embellishments as desired.
- Rubber band, if needed for securing embellishments.
- Floral foam and sheet moss, if desired.
- Ribbon or raffia, if desired.

Clear glass marbles (above) or preserved autumn leaves and dried naturals (opposite) are used for creative jar-in-a-jar candles.

TIPS FOR MAKING JAR-IN-A-JAR CANDLES

Secure jars with floral adhesive. Stack two inner jars, if necessary, to achieve desired height.

Secure items such as leaves or stems around jar, using rubber band; conceal rubber band with ribbon or raffia bow.

Conceal threaded tops of jars with ribbon, if desired.

GOLD-LEAF ACCESSORIES

Create elegant gilded accessories by applying a gold-leaf finish. For an easy and affordable way to achieve the look of real gold leaf, use an imitation gold leaf. Imitation silver-leaf and copper-leaf materials are also available. Applied in the traditional manner, gold leaf gives the shiny, gilded finish of the candlestick opposite, but an antiqued finish, shown on the bowl, can be achieved with an easy variation of the technique. The gold leaf can also be applied in stenciled design motifs, as on the urn.

MATERIALS

FOR ALL GOLD-LEAF FINISHES

- Imitation gold leaf and water-based gold-leaf adhesive, available at craft stores.
- Brush, for applying the gold-leaf adhesive.
- Clear finish or aerosol clear acrylic sealer.

FOR ANTIQUED FINISH

- Acrylic or flat latex paint in black or red, for base coat, and in black, for specking.
- 100-grit sandpaper; tack cloth.

FOR STENCILED DESIGNS

- Painter's masking tape.
- Sheet of glass; mat knife.

HOW TO APPLY A GOLD-LEAF FINISH

1 **Traditional gold-leaf finish.** Apply an even, light coat of the gold-leaf adhesive, using paintbrush; allow to set until clear, or about 1 hour; surface will be tacky, but not wet.

2 Cut sheet of imitation gold leaf into smaller pieces, no larger than one-fourth of a sheet, using scissors; hold the gold leaf between the supplied tissues and avoid touching it directly with your hands. Slide the bottom tissue from underneath gold leaf; touching the top tissue, press gold leaf in place over the adhesive.

(Continued)

3 Remove the top tissue. Using soft, dry paintbrush in an up-and-down motion, gently tamp the gold leaf in place to affix it. Then smooth gold leaf, using brush strokes.

4 Continue to apply additional pieces of the gold leaf, overlapping them slightly; the excess gold leaf will brush away.

5 Fill in any spaces or gaps between sheets of gold leaf, if desired, by applying adhesive and small pieces of gold leaf. Apply clear finish or aerosol clear acrylic sealer, to prevent marring and tarnishing.

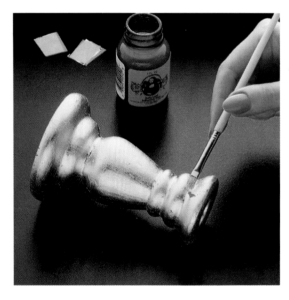

1 **Antiqued gold-leaf finish.** Apply a base coat of acrylic or flat latex paint in red or black; allow to dry. Apply gold-leaf adhesive and gold leaf, as in steps 1 to 3, page 81.

2 Scratch the surface after gold leaf has set for 1 hour, using folded piece of 100-grit sandpaper; this allows the base coat to show in some areas. Wipe surface with tack cloth to remove any grit.

3 Speck project with black paint, testing the technique first. Dip toothbrush into diluted black acrylic or flat latex paint; blot on paper towel. Run craft stick or finger along bristles of toothbrush to spatter specks of paint onto surface. Apply clear finish or aerosol clear acrylic sealer.

HOW TO APPLY STENCILED GOLD-LEAF DESIGNS

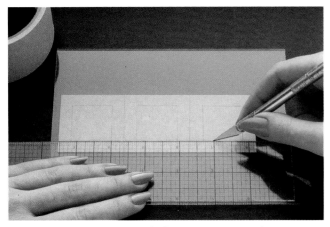

1 Cut self-adhesive stencils from painter's masking tape, by affixing a piece of painter's masking tape to a piece of glass and cutting out the desired shape, using a mat knife.

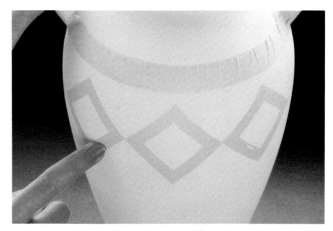

2 Prepare the surface to be embellished so it is smooth and clean. Remove the stencils from glass, and affix them to the prepared surface. Press tape firmly in place, making sure edges are secured.

3 Apply a light, even coat of gold-leaf adhesive to cutout areas, using small paintbrush; allow the adhesive to extend onto the tape. Allow adhesive to set until clear, for about 1 hour; the surface will be tacky, but not wet.

4 Cut a sheet of gold leaf slightly larger than stencil area; hold the gold leaf between supplied tissues, and avoid touching it directly with hands. Slide the bottom tissue from underneath the gold leaf; touching top tissue, press the gold leaf in place over the cutout area.

5 Remove the top tissue. Using soft, dry paintbrush in an up-and-down motion, gently tamp the gold leaf in place to affix it. Then smooth gold leaf, using brush strokes from the center of motif to edges; make sure gold leaf adheres well at edges.

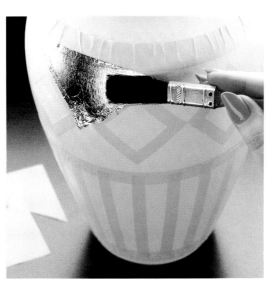

6 Trim gold leaf along edge of tape, using mat knife. Remove tape carefully. Apply aerosol clear acrylic sealer or clear finish to entire surface.

A charger is a large, decorative plate. Originally, wooden chargers were used under metal plates for carrying hot foods from the kitchen. Although chargers are sometimes still used for this purpose, they are more often used today for special occasions. In fine dining, a charger is placed at each place setting before the guests arrive at the table, and the plates for the soup, salad, and entrée are set on the charger. The chargers are then removed before the dessert course is served. This use of chargers began in the Victorian era when it was considered rude for a guest to be left without a plate between courses.

Chargers add color and interest to a table setting, enhancing the mood of any occasion. They vary in size from about 11" to 15" (28 to 38 cm). Select a size that is larger than the dinner plates you are using, so the rim of the charger will show around the edge of the plate.

Although some chargers may be costly, simple brass chargers are reasonably priced and can be sand-finished for a unique brushed effect. Unfinished wooden chargers can be purchased inexpensively from craft stores and woodworker's stores, then finished with color washing or gold leaf.

The instructions for sand-finished brass chargers and color-washed wooden chargers are on the following pages. To make the antiqued and stenciled gold-leaf chargers at right, see the instructions for gold leaf on pages 81 to 83.

Chargers *are used under soup, salad, and dinner plates in fine dining. They remain on the table throughout the dinner courses until the dessert is served. The brass charger opposite is sand-finished for a brushed appearance.*

Gold-leaf chargers *add elegance to the table setting. The instructions for the antiqued gold-leaf finish and the stenciled gold-leaf designs (above) are on pages 81 to 83.*

Color-washed wooden charger *(left) adds a cheerful accent to a country table setting.*

HOW TO SAND-FINISH A BRASS CHARGER

MATERIALS

- Brass charger.
- 60-grit sandpaper.

- Lint-free cloths.
- Aerosol clear acrylic sealer.

1 Scratch the surface of a brass charger, using 60-grit sandpaper in a random circular or curved motion.

2 Wash surface to remove any grit, and wipe dry, using lint-free cloths. Apply several light coats of aerosol clear acrylic sealer.

HOW TO APPLY COLOR-WASHED STRIPES TO A WOODEN CHARGER

MATERIALS

- Craft acrylic paints in desired colors.
- 100-grit, 150-grit, and 220-grit sandpaper.
- Tack cloth.

- Painter's masking tape.
- Sponge applicator.
- Clear finish or aerosol clear acrylic sealer.

1 Sand the charger in the direction of the wood grain, using 150-grit sandpaper, then 220-grit sandpaper. Remove any grit, using a tack cloth.

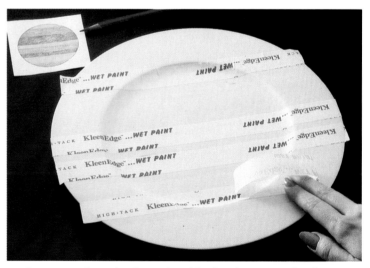

2 Determine desired color and width of each stripe in the charger, repeating colors as desired. Using painter's masking tape, mask off each side of stripes for first paint color.

3 Dilute paints, one part paint to two parts water. Apply the first paint color lightly to the masked stripes, using a sponge applicator; use paint sparingly. Allow to dry; remove tape.

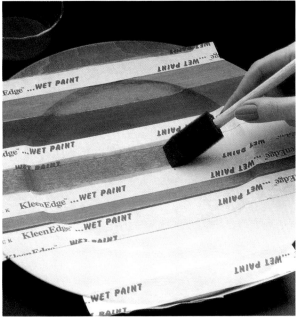

4 Repeat steps 2 and 3 for each remaining paint color, allowing paint to dry between colors.

6 Apply coat of clear finish or aerosol clear acrylic sealer to the charger. Apply additional coats as desired, sanding smooth between coats.

5 Sand painted charger in the direction of wood grain, using 100-grit sandpaper, to give a worn appearance to the surface, especially sanding along outer and inner edges of rim.

NAPKIN RINGS

Napkin rings can add the final touch to a place setting as they secure napkins into neat rolls, softly draped arrangements, or fanfolds. Several napkin rings can be assembled quickly and, since they require minimal materials, are inexpensive as well.

Unfinished wooden rings from craft and woodworker's stores can be embellished to create elegant tapestry-covered napkin rings or Western rings of suede and twigs. Make beaded napkin rings by stringing narrow decorative beads onto ribbon, cording, or leather lacing, or try some of the other creative ideas shown.

Western napkin ring (page 90) consists of fringed suede conchos, strips of leather, and twigs, held in place with a decorative upholstery tack.

Tapestry napkin ring (page 91) is trimmed with gimp, for an elegant look.

Beaded napkin ring (page 91) is quickly made by stringing decorative beads onto a length of metallic cording.

Old silverware (above) is bent into a circular form to create a clever napkin ring. Curve the silverware around a dowel or pipe, tapping it with a wooden mallet.

Seasonal cookie cutter (below), used as a napkin ring, becomes an instant holiday accessory.

Safety lollipops and candy bracelets, used with paper birthday napkins, are popular with children.

Personalized ribbon streamer (above) works well for birthdays and for other special occasions. The message can be added with paint pens or press-on letters.

Fresh flower and a ribbon (below) combine for a luxurious look. To keep the flower fresh, place the stem in a water tube, available from floral shops.

HOW TO MAKE A WESTERN NAPKIN RING

MATERIALS

- Unfinished wooden napkin ring.
- Craft acrylic paint in bronze metallic, for painting inside of the napkin ring.
- Scraps of heavy paper and suede.
- Fringed suede concho.
- Twig, cut about 3" (7.5 cm) long.
- Decorative upholstery tack.
- Thick white craft glue or fabric glue.

1 Sand napkin ring smooth. Apply bronze metallic paint to the inside and outside of the napkin ring; allow to dry. Apply bronze metallic paint to heavy paper. Cut narrow triangle from painted paper; set aside.

2 Cut strip of suede, ½" (1.3 cm) wide and 2" (5 cm) longer than circumference of napkin ring. Insert strip into openings of fringed concho, from right side; position the concho at center of the strip.

3 Insert twig between suede strip and concho; place the paper triangle from step 1 under strip. Secure triangle and suede strip to twig with decorative upholstery tack.

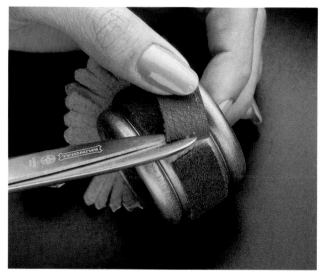

4 Wrap suede strip around napkin ring, securing it with glue; trim ends of the strip as necessary to butt them together on back of napkin ring.

HOW TO MAKE A TAPESTRY NAPKIN RING

MATERIALS

- Scraps of tapestry fabric.
- Gimp trim.
- Craft acrylic paint, for painting inside of the napkin ring.
- Unfinished wooden napkin ring.
- Thick white craft glue or fabric glue.

1 Sand napkin ring smooth. Apply paint to inside and edges of napkin ring. Cut strip of tapestry fabric to fit around napkin ring, about ½" (1.3 cm) narrower than width of ring.

2 Glue strip of tapestry to outside of ring, centering the strip; trim ends of the strip as necessary to butt them together. At ends, seal raw edges with glue.

3 Glue gimp trim around napkin ring, covering upper and lower edges of the fabric. Trim the ends of the gimp as necessary to butt them together on back of napkin ring, sealing ends of gimp with glue.

HOW TO MAKE A BEADED NAPKIN RING

MATERIALS

- Assorted decorative beads.
- 12" to 15" (30.5 to 38 cm) length of decorative cording, such as rayon or metallic cording or leather lacing.
- Beading needle, if necessary.

1 String the beads onto cording, covering 6" to 7" (15 to 18 cm) of the cording.

2 Knot ends of cording together on back of napkin ring, next to beads, and trim tails **(a).** Or, for another style, add beads to tails of cording on front of napkin ring **(b).**

PORCELAIN FLOWERS & BOWS

Silk or polyester flowers can be crafted to resemble porcelain flowers. Porcelain bows, made using the same technique, can be added to the arrangements.

The flowers are painted with a base coat of matte-finish white aerosol paint, which provides a good background for all colors and adds body to the flowers; it is not necessary to apply this base coat to the ribbon if white ribbon is used. To porcelainize the flowers and bows, they are dipped in a setting agent and painted with

acrylic paints. For the look of fine porcelain, thin the paint with extender. When extender is added, the paint spreads more smoothly.

Porcelain flowers and bows can decorate baskets or grapevine wreaths, or be used as an arrangement in a vase. Porcelain roses have a Victorian look, but other types of flowers may be used for other decorating styles, including contemporary.

MATERIALS

- Silk or polyester flowers; use flowers without plastic parts, or cover any plastic with florist's tape to ensure that paint will bond.
- Basket, grapevine wreath, or other object to be decorated.
- White ribbon for bows.
- Matte-finish white aerosol paint.
- Porcelain-setting agent.
- Acrylic paints in desired colors.

- Extender to thin the paint, optional.
- Clear aerosol glaze for porcelainizing; read cautions on label before use.
- Artist's brushes, #10 shader for ribbon; #8 flat or shader and #2 filbert or shader for flowers and leaves; #2 round for painting small details.
- Wire cutters for cutting flower stems; disposable plastic bowl for setting agent; disposable plate for paint palette.

Porcelain flowers and bows
embellish picture frames, lamps,
wreaths, or other room
accessories.

HOW TO MAKE PORCELAIN FLOWERS

1 Plan design of project, including bow. Pull blossoms and leaves from stem, or cut them, using wire cutter. Trim rough edges with small scissors. Spray each item with aerosol paint; allow to dry.

2 Pour setting agent into plastic bowl to depth necessary to dip flowers. Beginning with largest blossom, dip into setting agent. Strip off as much setting agent as possible by pulling petals gently between your forefinger and thumb.

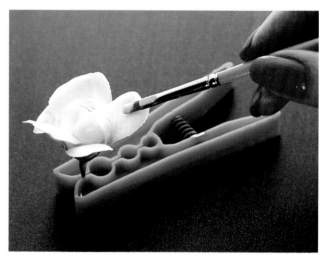

3 Arrange petals as desired. Remove any excess setting agent with flat artist's brush to achieve a smooth coating. Clamp or hang blossom until dry.

4 Repeat for remaining flowers, then leaves. Allow items to dry overnight.

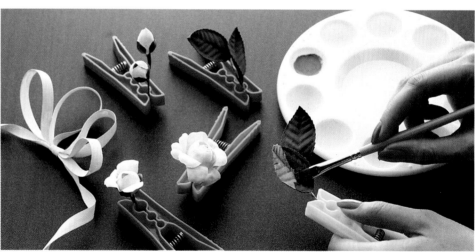

5 Thin acrylic paints with extender, if desired. Paint flowers, leaves, and porcelainized bow (opposite), shading if desired; allow to dry. Apply second coat of paint if brush strokes are noticeable; allow to dry.

6 Affix items to project, using setting agent and brush. Also apply setting agent to flowers, blossoms, and bow where items touch. Trim ends of ribbon.

7 Spray entire project with one or two coats of clear aerosol glaze.

HOW TO MAKE A PORCELAIN BOW

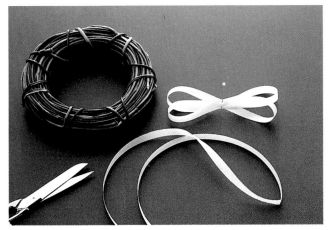

1 Loop ribbon in a figure eight, to determine desired size and number of loops; cut a piece of ribbon to this length. For knot and streamers, cut a second piece of ribbon to desired length.

2 Dip ribbons into setting agent, and pull through fingers to strip off as much as possible. Loop first ribbon in figure eight; place on table over second ribbon. Bring ends of second ribbon up over loops; tie.

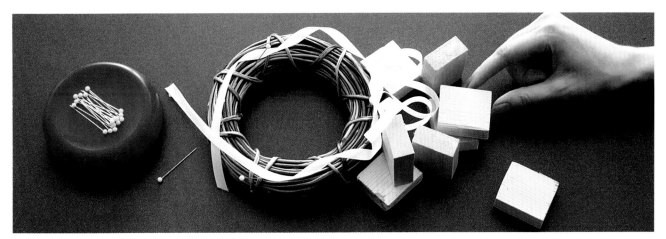

3 Arrange bow in desired position, draping and twisting loops and streamers. Support ribbon with props as necessary. Allow to dry overnight. Complete project as in steps 5 to 7 (opposite).

Table
Linens

BASIC TABLE LINENS

For variety, make a selection of basic tablecloths, including round, square, and oval styles, as well as placemats and napkins in several colors. By sewing your own tablecloths, you can make custom sizes and shapes for nonstandard tables, including oval tables.

For table linens, you may want to select durable, stain-resistant decorator fabrics that have been treated to repel soil and water. To avoid seaming large tablecloths, choose a wide fabric, such as one of the 72" (183 cm) tablecloth linens available at fabric stores. Or gain the extra width needed by adding a border to the tablecloth as on pages 109 to 111. Round tablecloths are frequently seamed, but the seam falls into the drape of the fabric along one side of the tablecloth, making it less noticeable.

For a greater selection of wide tablecloth fabrics, you can recut a ready-made purchased tablecloth to fit the actual size and shape of your table, instead of using a purchased fabric.

Determine the length and width of the tablecloth by measuring across the tabletop in both directions. Then add twice the desired *drop length,* or overhang, to this measurement. Drop lengths range from 8" (20.5 cm) to floor-length, with most drop lengths between 10" and 15" (25.5 and 38 cm).

Placemats range in size from 12" × 17" (30.5 × 43 cm) to 14" × 19" (35.5 × 48.5 cm). Finish them with a simple hem or edge finish as on pages 100 and 101. Or, for a more decorative look, select from the styles on pages 109 and 116.

Make napkins in a generous size, such as 15" (38 cm) square for luncheon napkins and 18" (46 cm) square for dinner napkins. Generously sized napkins offer liberal protection for the guests, and many napkin-folding techniques are more successful with the larger sizes.

All that is needed to make basic tablecloths, placemats, and napkins is to finish the edges. For simplicity, press a narrow hem in place, mitering the corners of squares and rectangles, and stitch the hem on the conventional sewing machine. Or finish the edges of the table linens with the 3-thread overlock stitch on a serger.

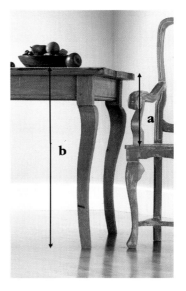

Drop length is the distance you want the tablecloth to hang over the edge of the table. Determine the exact drop length for your table by measuring. You may want the tablecloth to clear the chair seats and hang freely **(a);** this drop length will measure from 8" to 10" (20.5 to 25.5 cm). For a more formal look, use a longer drop length. Floor-length tablecloths **(b)** and tablecloths that drape onto the floor are especially elegant.

HOW TO CUT A ROUND TABLECLOTH

1 Measure the diameter of the round table; add twice the drop length, to determine the measurement for the finished tablecloth. Cut a square of fabric at least 1" (2.5 cm) larger than this size; piece two fabric widths together, if necessary, and press seam open. Fold square of fabric in half lengthwise and crosswise. Pin layers together.

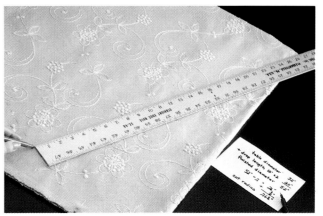

2 Divide measurement for the finished tablecloth by two and add ½" (1.3 cm), to determine radius of cut circle. Mark an arc, using straightedge and pencil, measuring from the folded center of fabric, a distance equal to radius. Cut on marked line through all layers.

HOW TO CUT AN OVAL OR CUSTOM-SHAPED TABLECLOTH

1 Measure the length and width of table at longest points; add twice the drop length. Cut a rectangle of fabric at least 1" (2.5 cm) larger than this size; piece the fabric widths together, if necessary, and press the seams open.

2 Place fabric on table, centered lengthwise and crosswise; weight fabric down. Measure and mark around tablecloth, an amount equal to the desired drop length plus ½" (1.3 cm). Cut on the marked line.

HOW TO NARROW-HEM TABLE LINENS USING THE CONVENTIONAL SEWING MACHINE

CUTTING DIRECTIONS

Cut the tablecloth, placemat, or napkin 1" (2.5 cm) larger than the desired finished size, piecing fabric widths together, if necessary, for large tablecloths.

1 **Rectangular or square linens.** Press under ½" (1.3 cm) on each side of fabric. Unfold corner; fold diagonally so pressed folds match. Press the diagonal fold; trim corner as shown.

2 Fold under the raw edge ¼" (6 mm). Press double-fold hem in place.

3 Stitch the hem close to inner fold, using straight stitch on conventional sewing machine and pivoting at corners; do not stitch along folds of miter.

1 **Round or oval linens.** Stitch around fabric circle or oval, a scant ¼" (6 mm) from raw edge. Fold and press the fabric along stitching line.

2 Fold and press fabric again to make a ¼" (6 mm) double-fold hem, easing in excess fabric. Stitch hem close to inner fold, using straight stitch on conventional machine.

HOW TO EDGE-FINISH TABLE LINENS USING A SERGER

1 Rectangular or square linens. Set the serger for balanced 3-thread overlock stitch, threading both the loopers of machine with woolly nylon thread, if desired, for best thread coverage; use regular thread in needle. Set the stitch width at 4 to 5 mm; set stitch length at 1 mm. Check the stitch quality on a sample of fabric; adjust the tension, if necessary.

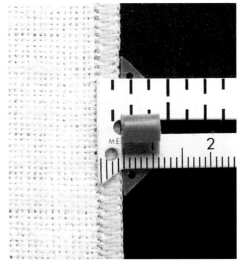

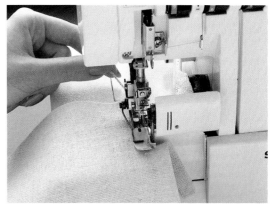

2 Stitch along one side of fabric, then opposite side, holding the tail chain taut as you begin stitching; trim away ½" (1.3 cm) with serger blade. Leave long tail chain at ends.

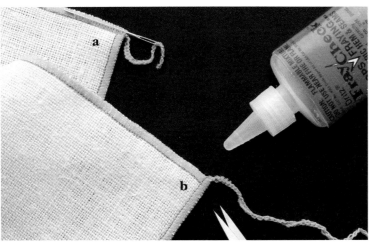

3 Stitch remaining two sides of fabric as in step 2. Thread the tail chain through eye of tapestry needle, and weave needle under overlock stitches for about 1" (2.5 cm) **(a);** cut off remaining length of tail chain. Or apply liquid fray preventer to stitches at corners **(b);** allow to dry, and cut off entire tail chain.

1 Round or oval linens. Set serger as in step 1, above. Stitch around the tablecloth, trimming ½" (1.3 cm) with the serger blade; at beginning, stitch onto edge of fabric at an angle.

2 Overlap the previous stitches for 1" (2.5 cm) at end. Lift presser foot, and shift fabric so it is behind needle. Stitch straight off edge of the fabric as shown; continue stitching to leave a long tail chain. (Presser foot was removed to show needle position.)

3 Apply liquid fray preventer to tail chain. Trim tail chain next to stitches.

101

TABLECLOTHS & PLACEMATS

Bordered table linens *include the tablecloth above, decorated with a painted check design, and several styles of placemats (opposite), some laminated and painted.*

Tablecloths and placemats with mitered borders have a simple style that works well for decorating kitchens. For more detailing, add fabric painting, like the check design shown here. By making your own tablecoverings, you can customize the sizes and choose from an unlimited selection of fabrics.

For a tablecloth, measure the table and decide on the desired drop length. A drop length of one-third or two-thirds the table height is attractive; the longer length is more formal. The mitered border may be of any width; the tablecloth above has a 6" (15 cm) border. Placemats may also vary in size. A good finished size for a placemat is 12" × 18" (30.5 × 46 cm), including the border.

For placemats that will be especially practical for everyday use, the fabric may be laminated. To clean the laminated placemats, just wipe them off with a damp cloth and allow them to air dry. Laminate the placemat fabric by using a cool-fuse paper-backed fusible adhesive, such as Heat 'n Bond®, which bonds a two-gauge clear vinyl to the right side of the fabric. Because the cool-fuse adhesive bonds at the silk setting of a dry iron, the vinyl adheres to the fabric without melting. The fabric pieces are laminated as on pages 106 and 107, before the mitered border is stitched.

When making painted and laminated placemats, do not use a decorator fabric that has a stain-resistant or water-resistant finish. These finishes often prevent fabric paints from adhering to the fabric and prevent the fusible adhesives from bonding well, causing a bubbled appearance. Placemats may be painted and then laminated, if desired. The fabric paint does not interfere with the bonding and does not smear.

HOW TO SEW A TABLECLOTH & PLACEMATS WITH A BORDER

MATERIALS

- Fabrics in two contrasting colors; for painted or laminated tablecoverings, avoid fabrics with stain-resistant or water-resistant finishes.
- Fabric paints and cellulose sponge to use as an applicator stamp, for painting check design.

- Cool-fuse paper-backed fusible adhesive, two-gauge clear vinyl, and silicone lubricant, for laminating placemat fabric.

CUTTING DIRECTIONS

If you are making laminated placemats, laminate the fabric as on pages 106 and 107 before cutting the pieces to the exact size. For a tablecloth or placemat, cut the middle panel to desired length and width plus ½" (1.3 cm), to allow for ¼" (6 mm) seam allowances. You will need four border strips, with the cut width equal to the desired finished width of the border plus 1¼" (3.2 cm). To determine the length of the border strips, add two times the cut width of the border plus 2" (5 cm) to the cut size of the middle panel; cut two border strips based on the width of the middle panel and two based on the length of the middle panel.

1 Apply painted check design to tablecloth or placemat fabric, if desired (page 106); laminate placemat fabric, if desired (pages 106 and 107). Mark middle panel at center of each side, on wrong side; mark center of each border strip on wrong side.

2 Mark the middle panel at all corners, ¼" (6 mm) from each raw edge, on wrong side of fabric.

3 Pin one border strip to one side of middle panel, right sides together, matching raw edges and centers.

4 Stitch border strip to middle panel in ¼" (6 mm) seam, starting and ending at corner markings.

5 Press seam allowances toward border. Fold the middle panel diagonally at corners, matching raw edges of border strips.

6 Place straightedge along fold; draw stitching line for mitered seam on border, using chalk or water-soluble marking pen.

7 Pin and stitch mitered seam, beginning at raw edge and ending at previous seamline.

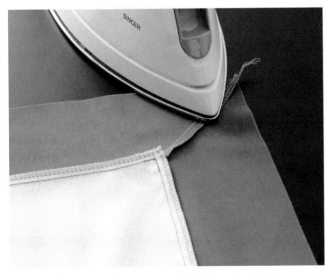

8 Trim the seam allowances to ¼" (6 mm); finish seam allowances. Press seam to one side.

9 Hem the outer edges by pressing under 1" (2.5 cm) on each side. Open the corner; fold diagonally so pressed folds match. Press; trim corner. Fold the raw edge under ½" (1.3 cm). Fold again on first foldline; press. Stitch hem.

HOW TO APPLY A PAINTED CHECK DESIGN

1 Cut cellulose sponge into squares of desired size, to use as stamps.

2 Cut fabric pieces for tablecloth or placemat (page 104). Tape fabric pieces to flat surface, within seam allowances.

3 Plan placement of design on fabric pieces, between the seam allowances. Pour a little fabric paint onto a small flat container. Dip sponge into paint. Apply to fabric.

4 Allow the paint to dry. Carefully remove tape from seam allowances of fabric. Heat-set paints, following manufacturer's directions. Laminate fabric pieces for the placemat, if desired (below).

HOW TO MAKE A LAMINATED PLACEMAT

CUTTING DIRECTIONS

Cut fabric pieces at least 1" (2.5 cm) larger than the required sizes for the placemat; cut two-gauge clear vinyl and cool-fuse paper-backed fusible adhesive ½" (1.3 cm) smaller than fabric pieces. The pieces will be trimmed to the correct size after they are laminated.

Test the laminating process on scraps of fabric, as in steps 1 to 4, to check the iron temperature and the length of time required for pressing. If the test sample appears milky or the vinyl does not adhere, raise the iron temperature slightly or press for longer time. If sample appears brittle or dry, the iron was too hot or pressing time was too long.

1 Paint a check design on the fabric, if desired (opposite). Center cool-fuse paper-backed fusible web on the right side of the fabric, with the adhesive side down. Fuse, following the manufacturer's directions. Avoid hot iron temperature and a long fusing time; in this step, it is only necessary to secure fabric lightly.

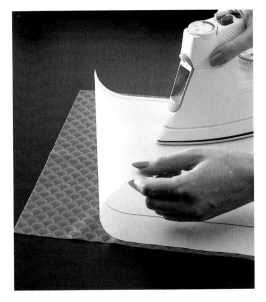

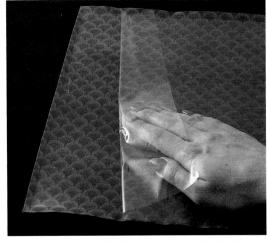

2 Remove paper backing after the fabric has cooled. Place clear vinyl over the fusible adhesive, smoothing out any wrinkles.

3 Cover vinyl with paper backing that was removed, with shiny side of paper against vinyl.

4 Press with dry iron at silk setting for 5 seconds. Lift iron and repeat as necessary until the entire surface is bonded. Save paper backing to use for pressing during construction.

5 Trim all sides of the laminated fabric, trimming pieces to the correct size for placemat.

6 Sew placemat (pages 104 and 105), using paper clips instead of pins to secure the fabric layers and stitching slowly; the seam finishes are not necessary. Topstitch and sew hems from the right side for a smooth appearance at needle holes; apply silicone lubricant to vinyl, to prevent skipped stitches.

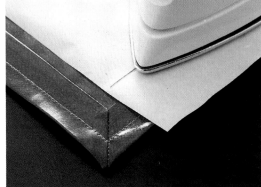

7 Press from vinyl side, using dry iron at silk setting; protect the vinyl by using the paper backing from fusible adhesive as a press cloth. Work quickly, to avoid overpressing. Remove any adhesive residue from right side, using a liquid spot remover or denatured alcohol.

Placemat *combines two coordinating tapestry fabrics and features border strips at the sides.*

TAPESTRY TABLE LINENS

Tapestry fabrics add simple elegance to table settings. Because tapestries often have intricate patterns, they work best for table linens of a straightforward design, such as the bordered tablecloths and placemats shown here. To simplify the construction and prevent excessive bulk at the edges, the tapestry tablecoverings are lined to the edge.

Select two coordinating tapestry fabrics, one for the center portion and one for the border strips. To reduce bulk, use muslin for the lining, or select a lightweight cotton in a color that matches the border fabric.

Determine the size of the center panel and the borders, based on your personal preference and on the design in the fabric you have selected. Because tapestries usually shrink a significant amount, steam press both the fabrics before cutting the pieces.

MATERIALS

- Two coordinating tapestry fabrics.
- Muslin or other lightweight cotton, for lining.

Tablecloth shows off a wide border, mitered at the corners.

HOW TO SEW A BORDERED TAPESTRY PLACEMAT

CUTTING DIRECTIONS

Determine the finished length and width of the placemat; placemats range in size from 12" × 17" (30.5 × 43 cm) to 14" × 19" (35.5 × 48.5 cm). To determine the cut size of the middle panel from side to side, subtract two times the desired finished width of the border; then add 1" (2.5 cm) to allow for two ½" (1.3 cm) seam allowances. The cut size of the middle panel from front to back is 1" (2.5 cm) longer than the desired finished size.

Cut two border strips, each 1" (2.5 cm) wider than the desired finished width of the border and 1" (2.5 cm) longer than the desired finished size of the placemat from front to back.

Cut the lining as in step 2, below, after the border has been applied.

1 Stitch border strips to the sides of middle panel, stitching ½" (1.3 cm) seams. Press seams open.

2 Cut the lining ¼" (6 mm) shorter than length and width of pieced top; this prevents the lining from showing on the right side at edges.

(Continued)

3 Pin the lining to the pieced top, right sides together, matching raw edges. With lining side up, stitch ½" (1.3 cm) seam on all four sides, taking one diagonal stitch across corners; leave an opening on one side for turning.

4 Trim seam allowances diagonally across the corners; apply liquid fray preventer. Press the lining seam allowance toward lining. Turn right side out; press. Hand-stitch opening closed.

HOW TO SEW A BORDERED TAPESTRY TABLECLOTH

CUTTING DIRECTIONS

Determine the finished length and width of the tablecloth, including the drop length, as on page 99. To determine the cut size of the middle panel, subtract two times the desired finished width of the border from the finished length and width of the tablecloth; then add 1" (2.5 cm), to allow for ½" (1.3 cm) seam allowances.

You will need four border strips, with the cut width equal to the desired finished width of the border plus 1" (2.5 cm). To determine the length of the border strips, add two times the cut width of the border plus 2" (5 cm) to the cut side of the middle panel; cut two border strips based on the width of the middle panel and cut two based on the length of the middle panel.

Cut the lining as in step 9, opposite, after the border has been applied.

1 Mark middle panel at center of each side, on wrong side; mark center of each border strip on wrong side.

2 Mark the middle panel at all corners, ½" (1.3 cm) from each raw edge, on wrong side of fabric.

3 Pin one border strip to one side of middle panel, right sides together, matching raw edges and centers.

4 Stitch border strip to middle panel in ½" (1.3 cm) seam, starting and ending at corner markings.

5 Fold middle panel diagonally at corners, matching border seams and raw edges of border strips. Place a straightedge along the fold; draw stitching line for mitered seam on border, using chalk. Stitching line should be at 45° angle to raw edge.

6 Pin and stitch mitered seam, beginning at raw edge and ending at previous seamline.

7 Trim the seam allowances on mitered corners to ½" (1.3 cm). Trim the middle panel diagonally across corners of border seam. Apply liquid fray preventer to trimmed edges, to prevent raveling.

8 Clip the seam allowances of border strips at corners. Apply liquid fray preventer. Press all seams open.

9 Cut the lining ½" (1.3 cm) shorter than the length and width of the pieced top; this prevents the lining from showing on the right side at the edges. Finish tablecloth as for placemat, steps 3 and 4, opposite.

BULLION FRINGE
TABLE LINENS

Bullion fringe adds elegance to table linens. It may be stitched around the edges of tablecloths or along the short, angled ends of a table runner. Bullion fringe is available in acetate, rayon, cotton, and metallic as well as in a variety of fringe lengths. Because the heading of the fringe ravels quickly, always apply liquid fray preventer to the area that will be cut and allow it to dry before cutting the fringe.

***Round tablecloth** has a luxurious look when trimmed with bullion fringe. At left, an oversized tablecloth falls elegantly onto the floor.*

Table runner *with fringed ends drapes gracefully over the table. The ends of the table runner are angled to add interest.*

Small square tablecloth *with bullion fringe edging is placed on the table at an angle.*

HOW TO SEW A ROUND TABLECLOTH WITH BULLION FRINGE

1 Determine desired drop length for the tablecloth; subtract length of fringe, excluding the heading. Add twice this measurement to diameter of the round tabletop, to determine the diameter of fabric circle. Cut a square of fabric at least this size; piece two fabric widths together, if necessary, and press seam open. Fold square of fabric in half lengthwise and crosswise. Pin layers together.

2 Divide measurement for diameter of fabric circle by two, to determine radius. Mark an arc, using straightedge and pencil, measuring from folded center of fabric, a distance equal to radius. Cut on marked line through all layers.

3 Stitch around outer edge of fabric circle, using zigzag or overlock stitch; if using overlock stitch, do not trim edge of fabric. Pin the bullion fringe to fabric, with bottom of heading along edge of fabric; steam press as necessary to shape heading around curve.

4 Fold under ¾" (2 cm) at ends of heading; butt folded ends. Straight-stitch along top and bottom of heading.

HOW TO SEW A RECTANGULAR OR SQUARE TABLECLOTH WITH BULLION FRINGE

1 Determine the desired drop length for the tablecloth; subtract length of fringe, excluding the heading. Add twice this measurement to length and width of the tabletop, to determine cut size of fabric. Piece the fabric widths together, if necessary, and press seams open.

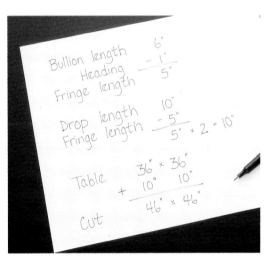

2 Stitch around all edges of the fabric, using zigzag or overlock stitch; if using overlock stitch, do not trim edge of fabric. Pin bullion fringe to fabric, with bottom of heading along edge of fabric, starting at middle of one side.

114

HOW TO SEW A TABLE RUNNER WITH BULLION FRINGE

1 Determine the cut length of the table runner as for length of rectangular tablecloth, step 1, opposite. Cut a rectangle from the face fabric, 16" (40.5 cm) wide and to determined cut length; cut rectangle from the lining, 15¾" (40 cm) wide and to the same length as the face fabric. Pin the rectangles, right sides together, matching the raw edges on the long sides. Stitch ½" (1.3 cm) on long edges. Turn right side out; press.

2 Mark one end of runner on long and short sides, 5" (25.5 cm) from corners. Draw lines diagonally across corners, between the marked points. Trim on marked lines. Repeat for other end of runner. Serge or zigzag layers together.

3 Pin the bullion fringe to the short ends, with the bottom of the heading along edge of fabric. Shape heading at corners, easing in fullness.

4 Fold under ¾" (2 cm) at ends of heading. Straight-stitch along top and bottom of heading, pivoting at corners.

3 Miter corners by tucking excess heading on left side of corner under the fold in the heading on right side; this will keep the heading from catching in the toes of presser foot as you sew.

4 Fold under ¾" (2 cm) at ends of heading; butt the folded ends. Straight-stitch along the top and bottom of heading. Turn the handwheel manually to stitch over the thick areas at folded ends and corners.

HEXAGONAL PLACEMATS

Hexagonal in shape, these placemats are a welcome change of pace from the usual rectangular placemats. Mitered braid or ribbon adds a simple border on the pointed sides, calling attention to the unique shape of the placemat.

For a coordinated look, use these placemats with triangle-point valances in the dining room. Buttons and tassels may be added to the center points at the sides as a finishing touch.

HOW TO SEW A HEXAGONAL PLACEMAT

MATERIALS (for four placemats)

- 1 yd. (0.95 m) fabric, for placemat tops.
- 1 yd. (0.95 m) fabric, for placemat backs.
- 4½ yd. (4.15 m) braid, grosgrain ribbon, or other tightly woven flat trim.
- Two buttons and two tassels for each placemat, if desired.

CUTTING DIRECTIONS

Make the pattern for the placemat as in step 1. For each placemat, cut one placemat top and one placemat back, using the pattern. Steam press the trim to preshrink it; cut two 20" (51 cm) lengths.

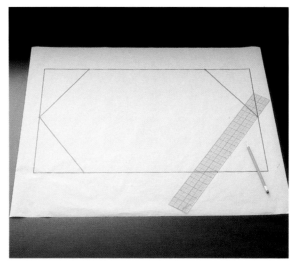

1 Draw 15" × 23" (38 × 58.5 cm) rectangle. Mark center of each short side. On long sides, mark points 5" (12.5 cm) from the corners. Draw the cutting lines from center marks on short sides to marked points on long sides. Cut pattern.

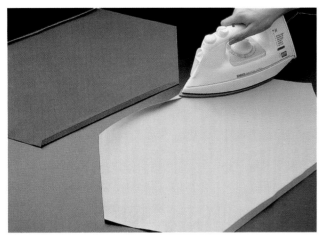

2 Cut one placemat top and one placemat back, using pattern. Press under ½" (1.3 cm) on upper and lower edges of both pieces.

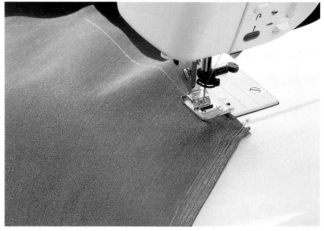

3 Pin placemat top and placemat back, right sides together, along pointed sides, matching raw edges; align folds on upper and lower edges. Stitch ½" (1.3 cm) seams on pointed sides.

4 Clip diagonally across corner. Press the seam allowances of the placemat back toward placemat back. Turn right side out, and press seamed edges.

5 Pin the trim to sides of placemat top, matching outer edges of trim and placemat. At points, mark the trim at edges, for miters.

6 Remove trim. With trim folded right sides together, stitch miters from mark at inner corner to mark at outer edge.

7 Trim mitered seam to ¼" (6 mm), leaving the outer point untrimmed.

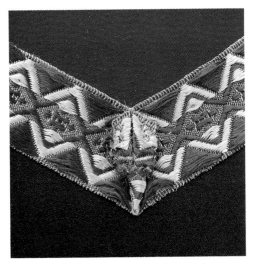

8 Press the seam open, and press the point flat.

9 Pin trim to placemat top. Fold ends at upper and lower edges between placemat top and placemat back; press.

11 Stitch buttons at points of trim, if desired. Secure the loop of the tassel around the button.

10 Pin placemat top and placemat back together along the upper and lower edges. Edgestitch around entire placemat, stitching trims in place. Edgestitch along inner edges of trims.

CROSS-STITCHED LINENS

Cross-stitching on linen is easy, and the results are beautiful. This simple craft lends itself to a number of kitchen accessories, including table linens and cafe curtains. On the accessories shown here, latticework is entwined with grapevines. The design (page 122) can be stitched in three different color combinations, for grape clusters of purple, red, and green.

The sewing method of cross-stitching, rather than the usual stab method, is used for linen. With the sewing method, the needle is taken up and down in one stroke, making it faster to stitch on linen than on other fabrics.

Cross-stitch designs are usually stitched over two threads of the linen. To determine the finished size of a design, divide the number of squares in the charted design by one-half the thread count of the fabric.

The centers of the horizontal and vertical rows of the charted design are indicated by arrows. Also indicated by arrows are the points at the ends of the design where the pattern begins to repeat itself; use these indicators when you want to continue to cross-stitch a border of lattice along the lower edge of a curtain panel or around a rectangular placemat.

Although linen is an evenweave fabric, it does have a distinct appearance in the lengthwise and crosswise grainlines. When working on linen, hold the fabric so the selvages run vertically and the crosswise grain runs horizontally. If the selvages have been removed, determine the grainline by pulling out one of the threads in each direction; the crosswise threads are the straightest.

When working with a bright color of embroidery floss that is not colorfast, rinse the skein in cool water until water runs clear, and allow the floss to dry thoroughly. To determine the number of strands of embroidery floss to use, the diameter of the floss to be threaded through the needle should be at least the diameter of one thread pulled from the fabric. Use a blunt-point tapestry needle in a size large enough to be easily threaded with the number of strands of floss you are using; sizes 24 and 26 are commonly used.

MATERIALS

- Linen of desired thread count.
- Embroidery floss in desired colors.
- Blunt-point tapestry needle in size 24 or 26.

Cafe curtains *(right) made of linen feature latticework and purple grapes. For the larger design, the stitches are worked over four threads in the linen, using four strands of embroidery floss.*

Placemat and napkin *(opposite) are made from 32-count linen, worked with two strands of embroidery floss. The lattice design with multicolored clusters of grapes trims one side of the placemat, while a single cluster of red grapes accents a corner of the napkin. Both are finished with narrow hems.*

Bread warmer *(below) has a cross-stitched corner motif. These grapes are worked in shades of green on 26-count linen, using two strands of floss. For an easy edge finish, machine-stitch ½" (1.3 cm) from the edges and pull the threads from each side to make fringe.*

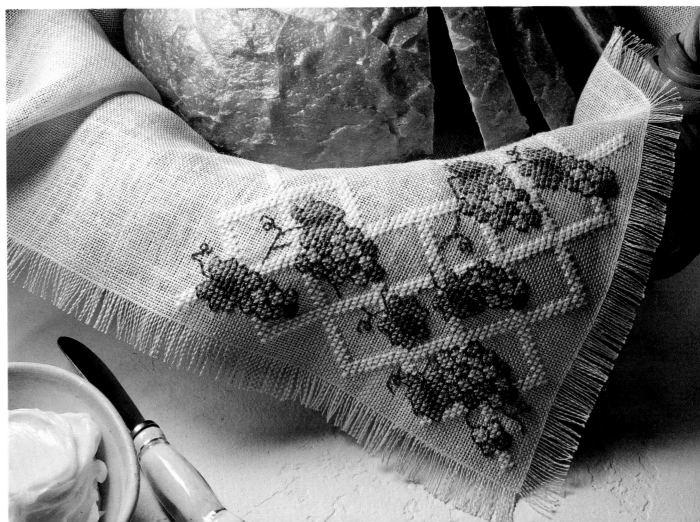

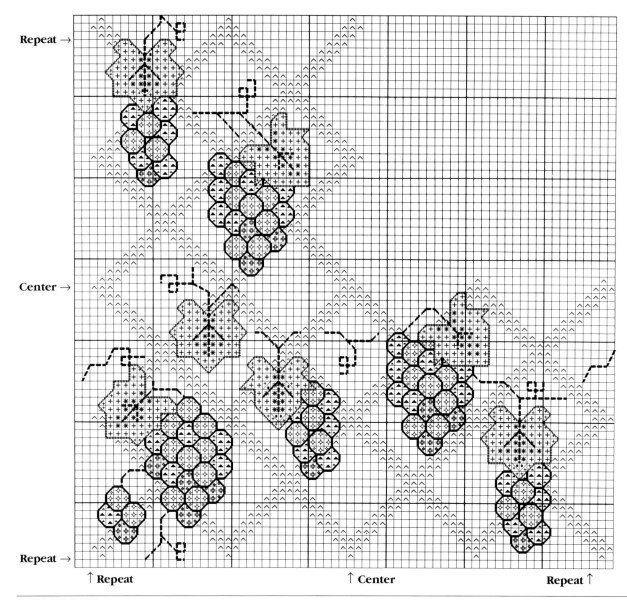

Repeat →

Center →

Repeat →

↑ **Repeat**   ↑ **Center**   **Repeat** ↑

DESIGN KEY

FOR LATTICE & VINES	FOR GREEN GRAPES	FOR PURPLE GRAPES	FOR RED GRAPES
∧ DMC white.	✧ DMC 472 lt. green.	✧ DMC 554 lt. purple.	✧ DMC 335 lt. red.
+ DMC 988 lt. green.	▲ DMC 471 med. green.	▲ DMC 553 med. purple.	▲ DMC 309 med. red.
✳ DMC 986 dk. green.	⌗ DMC 469 dk. green.	⌗ DMC 552 dk. purple.	⌗ DMC 498 dk. red.
⸽⸽⸽⸽⸽ DMC 986 backstitch.	— DMC 936 backstitch.	— DMC 550 backstitch.	— DMC 814 backstitch.
▬ ▬ ▬ DMC 300 backstitch.			

TIPS FOR CROSS-STITCHING

Cut the linen so at least 3" (7.5 cm) is allowed on each side of the design. Zigzag around the edges of the linen before you cross-stitch, to prevent raveling.

Fold the fabric in half lengthwise, then crosswise, to find the center; pin-mark. Find this point on the chart, using the arrow guidelines.

Cut embroidery floss into 36" (91.5 cm) lengths, to be folded in half when threading the needle. Separate the strands; recombine the number of strands needed.

Keep the needle 2" to 3" (5 to 7.5 cm) from one end of the floss; if the floss becomes worn next to the needle, it will not be noticeable in the cross-stitching.

Achieve a smoothly stitched surface by crossing all stitches in the same direction.

Skip up to six fabric threads, or three stitches, without breaking the embroidery floss, in order to continue a row of stitches in the same color; do not carry the floss over an area that will remain unstitched.

Unthread the needle to correct mistakes made a few stitches back; pull out the stitches, and restitch them correctly. For larger mistakes, clip the floss to remove the stitches.

Avoid tangling the floss by dropping the needle every few stitches and allowing the floss to untwist.

HOW TO CROSS-STITCH ON LINEN

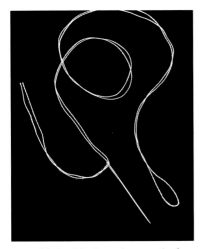

1 Fold double-length strand of embroidery floss in half; thread ends through the needle.

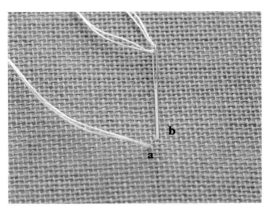

2 Bring the needle up through linen. Make half of the first cross-stitch, beginning **(a)** and ending **(b)** where a vertical linen thread crosses over horizontal thread; this supports stitch on linen. When first stitch is correctly positioned, entire design will be correct.

3 Thread needle through loop on wrong side of linen. Pull floss until loop is snug.

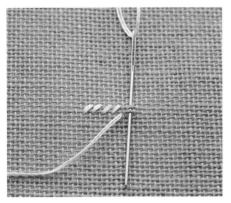

4 Work across the horizontal row to make first half of stitches, working each stitch over two linen threads; in one stroke, insert the needle at top of stitch and bring it up at bottom. Make one stitch for each symbol on chart.

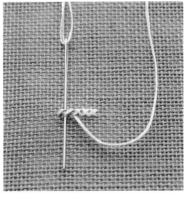

5 Work back over horizontal row to make second half of the cross-stitches, continuing to insert needle at top of stitch and bring it up at bottom.

6 Work rows in a downward direction, to bring the needle down in occupied hole and up in empty hole; this anchors stitches and keeps them smooth. You can turn fabric and chart upside down, if necessary.

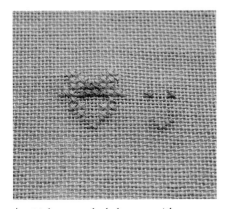

7 Make rounded shapes with one-quarter and three-quarter stitches, as indicated in chart. (Extra stitches were added to show detail.)

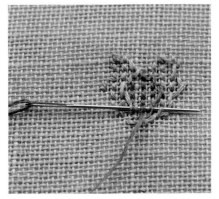

8 End stitching for each color or length of floss by bringing floss through to wrong side to complete last stitch. Run floss under several stitches on wrong side. Clip floss close to linen; do not knot floss.

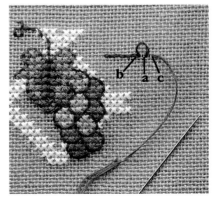

9 Outline details, using backstitch, as indicated on chart and on color key by colored straight lines; make backstitches as shown **(a, b, c)**.

SILVERWARE HOLDERS

Neatly arrange the silverware at a buffet in a silverware holder. The holder, either with or without lace trim, is divided into twenty-four compartments that separate the silverware for each guest. Constructed from four layered semicircles of fabric, the holder has radiating stitching lines that divide it into eighths, creating three rows of silverware compartments. For silverware with heavy handles, divide the holder into sixths instead of eighths, making eighteen larger compartments.

MATERIALS

- ¾ yd. (0.7 m) fabric.
- 6½ yd. (5.95 m) gathered lace trim, 2½" to 3" (6.5 to 7.5 cm) wide, optional.

Silverware holder may have a simple, tailored look as shown above. Or, for a more Victorian look, add lace trim as shown at left.

HOW TO MAKE A SILVERWARE HOLDER WITH LACE TRIM

1 Draw four semicircles on tracing paper, one each with a radius of 6", 8", 10", and 12" (15, 20.5, 25.5, and 30.5 cm). On the straight sides, add ½" (1.3 cm) seam allowance. Cut one semicircle of each size from fabric. The pieces will be referred to as A, B, C, and D, from the smallest to the largest.

2 Mark all fabric pieces on center of each straight side. On Piece B, lightly mark an arc 2" (5 cm) from center point; on Piece C, lightly mark an arc 4" (10 cm) from center point.

(Continued)

HOW TO MAKE A SILVERWARE HOLDER WITH LACE TRIM
(CONTINUED)

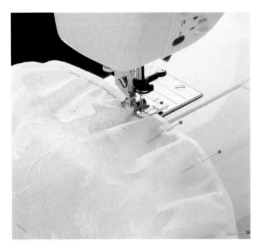

3 Pin lace trim to curved edge of Pieces A, B, and C, with right sides together and gathered edge of the lace along outer edge of fabric; match ends of lace trim to straight side of semicircle. Stitch just inside the gathered heading of lace trim.

4 Turn lace right side up; press seam allowances toward fabric. From the right side, topstitch ⅛" (3 mm) from seamline.

5 Repeat steps 3 and 4 for Piece D, folding a narrow double-fold hem at ends of the lace; begin and end the lace trim ½" (1.3 cm) from straight edge of semicircle.

6 Place Piece B over Piece C, right sides up, with straight edges even and matching center points. Pin and stitch along marked arc on Piece B.

7 Place Piece A over Piece B, right sides up, with the straight edges even and matching center points. Place Piece D over Piece A, right side up, with straight edges even and matching center points. Pin through all layers along straight edge.

8 Stitch ½" (1.3 cm) seam on the straight side. Press the seam open.

9 Turn Piece D to the back of the silverware holder; press in place.

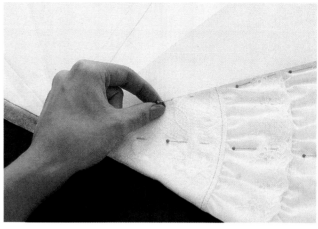

10 Fold back the top two layers to reveal the marked arc on Piece C; pin along arc through bottom two layers. Stitch along arc, beginning and ending at lower seam; take care not to catch top two layers in stitching.

11 Fold pattern for Piece D in half, then into quarters and eighths. Transfer the markings from the pattern to Piece D, using pins. This marks the dividing lines for the silverware compartments.

12 Stitch along the first marked line from the outer edge to the center point. Pivot at center point and stitch back to the outer edge along the opposite marked line. Repeat for two more sets of pressed lines. Stitch the last marked line from center point to outer edge.

13 Embellish the center point of the holder as desired with a bow, lace motif, or flowers. Insert silverware into layered compartments.

HOW TO MAKE A SILVERWARE HOLDER WITHOUT LACE TRIM

1 Follow steps 1 and 2 on page 125, except cut 8", 10", 12", and 14" (20.5, 25.5, 30.5, and 35.5 cm) semicircles. Stitch along the curved edges of all the semicircles, using overlock or zigzag stitch; press under ¼" (6 mm), and topstitch in place.

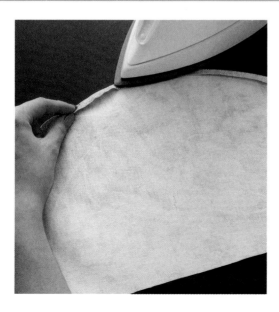

2 Follow steps 6 to 13, opposite. Clip the seam allowance on Piece D next to curved edge of Piece C; fold to the back, and hem.

TRAY DOILIES

For a custom look, make a lace-trimmed doily to fit a silver, brass, or wooden serving tray. Select fine linen or cotton fabric for a crisp doily that launders well. When selecting lace trim for an oval or round doily, keep in mind that narrow laces and laces with scallops or points on the outer edge are easier to shape around curves.

MATERIALS

- Lightweight linen or cotton fabric.
- Flat lace edging with one straight and one scalloped edge; allow extra yardage for shaping along curves or mitering corners.

HOW TO SEW A TRAY DOILY WITH CURVED SIDES

1 Place tracing paper over the tray; trace around rim of the tray with a pencil, to make pattern. Using pattern, cut fabric to finished size of doily.

2 Sew a gathering row along the straight edge of lace, if lace does not have a gathering thread in the heading.

3 Pin the lace edging to the doily fabric, aligning outer edge of lace to the outer edge of fabric. Pull the gathering thread to shape the inner edge of lace around the curve; overlap the ends of lace ⅜" (1 cm). Steam press.

4 Stitch along the inner, straight edge of lace, beginning at the center of the overlap, using narrow zigzag stitch.

5 Trim the fabric underneath the lace, ⅛" (3 mm) from stitching. At the overlap, stitch through both layers of lace, and trim excess lace close to stitching.

HOW TO SEW A TRAY DOILY WITH STRAIGHT SIDES

1 Make pattern and cut fabric for a tray with straight sides, such as a rectangular tray, as in step 1, opposite. Plan the lace placement so corners will miter attractively; it may not be possible to miter all corners alike.

2 Cut the lace edging into lengths slightly longer than each side. Pin lace edging to doily fabric, aligning the outer edge of the lace to the outer edge of the fabric.

3 Stitch along inner, straight edges of lace, using narrow zigzag. Trim the fabric underneath the lace. Stitch through both layers of lace from inner corner to outer corner; trim excess lace close to the stitching.

HARDANGER EMBROIDERY

Hardanger embroidery, with its geometric designs, blends well with most decorating schemes. Hardanger designs are easy to follow and to adapt. Most designs can be stitched by following a close-up photograph.

The embroidery is worked on 22-count Hardanger fabric. This basket-weave fabric is composed of a pattern of squares; each square is made of two strands. Traditionally, pieces were stitched on white fabric with white thread; however, variations combine different colors of fabric and thread.

Learning a few basic Hardanger stitch patterns enables you to create a variety of pieces. You may want to practice the stitches on a small sample before you begin a project. The Hardanger embroidery shown here illustrates various stitch patterns. The finished piece measures 8½" (21.8 cm) square, a suitable size for a first project.

The satin-stitch block is the primary stitch pattern; each block consists of five stitches over four fabric squares. The blocks can be stitched in a variety of patterns, such as a staircase effect or motifs with cutwork. The buttonhole stitch, a variation of the satin-stitch block, forms the edging for many projects. The star motif is also a satin-stitch block variation. Cutwork blocks are stitched using wrapping and web stitches. Satin-stitch blocks, buttonhole stitches, and star motifs are worked

using #5 pearl cotton and a size 22 tapestry needle. Work the wrapping and web stitches for cutwork blocks using #8 pearl cotton and a size 24 tapestry needle.

MATERIALS

- 22-count cotton Hardanger fabric.
- Pearl cotton, #5 and #8.
- Tapestry needles, sizes 22 and 24.
- Sharp, fine-pointed scissors.

TIPS FOR WORKING HARDANGER EMBROIDERY

Practice the stitches, using a contrasting thread, before starting a project.

Check your work often to make sure blocks are properly aligned with the weave of the fabric.

Leave 3" (7.5 cm) thread tails, securing them by weaving the ends under completed stitches on the wrong side of the piece.

Clip threads, rather than carry them; the wrong side of the piece should appear as neat as the right side.

Cut fabric for cutwork by cutting only on the side where the stitches have entered the fabric; never cut parallel to a satin-stitch block.

Hardanger stitch patterns include cutwork motifs *(a)*, satin-stitch blocks *(b)*, star motifs *(c)*, and buttonhole stitches *(d)*. The stitches are worked counting the fabric squares, according to a close-up photograph.

HOW TO STITCH THE HARDANGER SAMPLER PROJECT

1 Cut one 12" (30.5 cm) square of fabric, folding it in quarters to find center of fabric; finger-press. Stitch the center motif of satin-stitch blocks (opposite), starting at a corner about 2½" (6.5 cm) from the center.

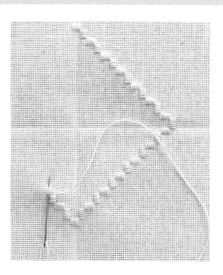

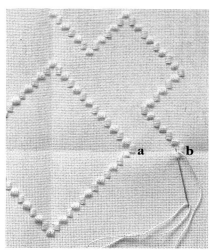

2 Stitch the outer satin-stitch block design; there are 28 squares between the corner block of the center motif **(a)** and the corresponding block of the outer design **(b).** Check work frequently to see that blocks are correctly aligned with the weave of the fabric.

3 Finish design by stitching the outer row of buttonhole stitches, opposite.

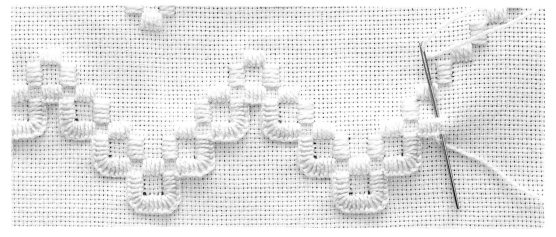

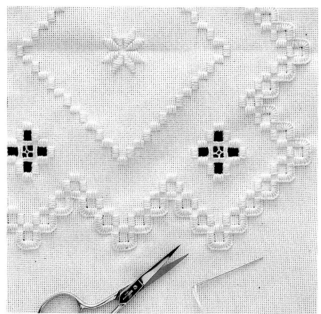

4 Stitch the center star motif (page 135). Stitch cutwork motifs (page 134), using wrapping stitch; add web stitch to center of each cutwork block, if desired.

5 Finish the edges of the Hardanger project as on page 135.

HOW TO MAKE SATIN-STITCH BLOCKS

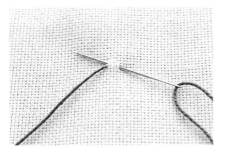 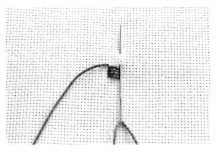 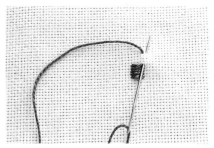

1 Bring needle up and count over four squares; insert the needle, bringing the needle out one square above where thread entered fabric.

2 Stitch to complete first five-stitch block; on fifth stitch, pivot needle and bring needle up four squares away.

3 Insert needle in the corner hole of previous block to make first stitch of second block.

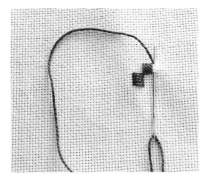 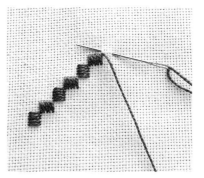

4 Complete five stitches for the second block; turn second corner by bringing needle up in same hole as last stitch.

5 Repeat from step 1 for the desired number of satin-stitch blocks, turning corners for desired design.

HOW TO MAKE BUTTONHOLE STITCHES

1 Bring needle up four squares from satin-stitch block. Insert at corner of block and bring out at thread entry, with thread looped under needle. Stitch four additional parallel stitches, looping thread under needle each time.

2 Stitch three diagonal stitches, using the corner hole of the fifth parallel stitch for each diagonal stitch; this forms rounded, outside corner.

 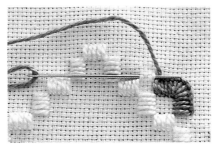 

3 Stitch the first parallel stitch of the second block, using the same corner hole.

4 Stitch five stitches of second block; at completion of fifth stitch, pivot needle, and stitch across four squares, bringing it up in corner hole of the fifth stitch; this will become the inside corner.

5 Repeat from step 1 for desired number of buttonhole stitches, turning outside and inside corners for desired design. When you run out of thread, start using a new length of thread at an inside corner.

HOW TO MAKE A CUTWORK MOTIF

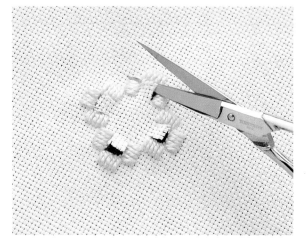

1 Wrapping stitch. Stitch a motif of 12 satin-stitch blocks. Carefully cut the fabric as shown; fabric is cut only on the side where the stitches have entered the fabric, never parallel to a satin-stitch block.

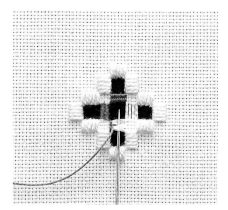

2 Remove all clipped threads from the fabric.

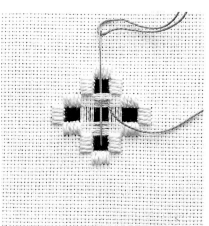

3 Secure thread on wrong side of fabric, and bring needle up through middle of the four unwoven fabric threads. Bring needle around one side and up through the middle.

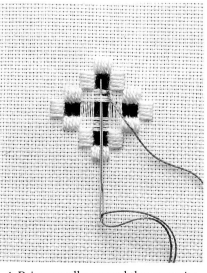

4 Bring needle around the opposite side and up through the middle.

1 Web stitch. Follow steps 1 to 5, above, wrapping one-half of the fourth side; insert needle up through center of adjacent bar, creating first web section.

5 Continue wrapping thread in a figure-eight pattern, pulling each stitch tightly. At completion of first bar, bring needle up through middle of next bar, and repeat to wrap all four sides; if web is desired, wrap one-half of the fourth side.

2 Insert needle under web section, then up into next bar.

3 Repeat at third bar. Complete the web by bringing needle over and around first web section. Insert needle up into center of uncompleted bar; finish wrapping the bar.

HOW TO MAKE A STAR MOTIF

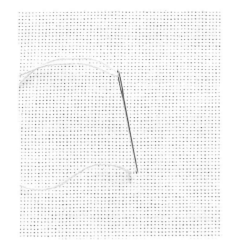

1 Locate center hole for star (as indicated by dot), and count up two squares; bring needle up. Work first satin stitch over two squares.

2 Stitch four additional stitches, increasing the length of each stitch on the right side by one square; fifth stitch covers six squares.

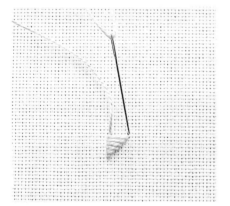

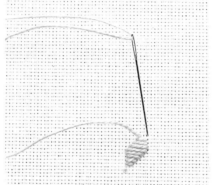

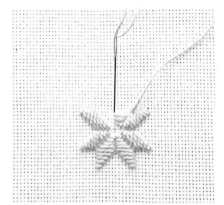

3 Work next stitch by decreasing length on left side by one stitch; stitch remains parallel with previous stitch on the right side.

4 Stitch three additional stitches, decreasing the length of each stitch on left side by one square; ninth stitch covers two squares.

5 Insert needle under stitches on wrong side; continue to make eight spokes, working from center out; adjoining spokes share holes. Star is worked in mirror-image pairs.

HOW TO FINISH THE EDGES OF A HARDANGER PROJECT

1 Machine-stitch around the border of the design, stitching just inside the ridge of the buttonhole stitch; use short stitch length and lightweight matching thread. (Contrasting thread was used to show detail.)

2 Trim as close as possible to buttonhole edge, using sharp scissors and taking care not to clip the pearl cotton thread.

MORE IDEAS FOR HARDANGER EMBROIDERY

Placemat, *adapted from an heirloom Hardanger design, is worked on a 16"× 20" (40.5 × 51 cm) rectangle of fabric; the finished size is 12¼"× 16" (31.2 × 40.5 cm). The design consists of satin-stitch blocks, buttonhole stitches, and half-star motifs. Cutwork has been done on the inner satin-stitch blocks, as on page 134. Work the design, counting squares in the fabric and the stitches in the actual-size photograph below.*

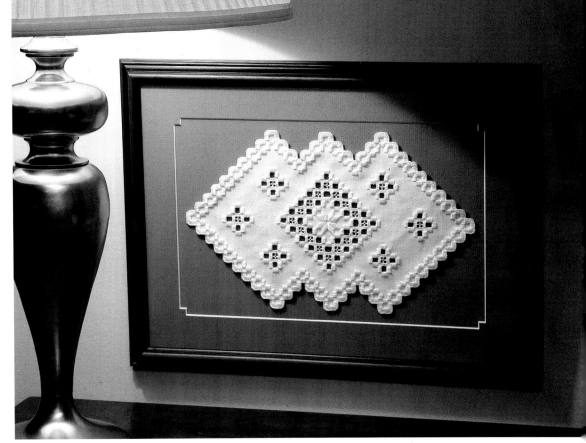

Framed doily is mounted on a dark background to highlight the cutwork. Worked on an 11" × 15" (28 × 38 cm) rectangle of fabric, the finished size is 7½" × 11½" (19.3 × 29.3 cm). The design consists of satin-stitch blocks, buttonhole stitches, and cutwork and star motifs. Work the design, counting the fabric squares and stitches in the actual-size photograph below.

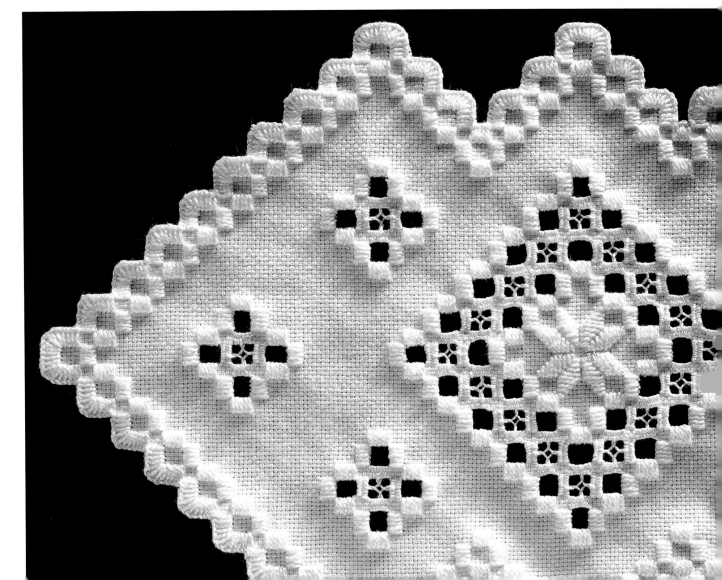

PLACE CARDS

Gift-wrapping paper, cut into various shapes, is glued to a place card.

Paper fan (below), folded accordion-style, embellishes this place card.

Wheat (above) or dried flowers can be secured to a place card with hot glue. Add a strip of art paper for more detail.

Place cards are used to indicate a compatible seating arrangement planned by the host or hostess. For formal occasions, such as weddings and banquets, place cards often reflect seating protocol, such as who sits at the head table and in what order. For less formal occasions, place cards can help guests find their seats quickly, while the host and hostess attend to last-minute details. For any special occasion, creative place cards can become decorative table appointments and personalize each place setting.

Place cards are easily made from simple items, such as construction paper, ribbon, dried flowers, and lace. Choose embellishments for the place cards that are in keeping with the theme or overall mood of the event.

HOW TO CUT A PLACE CARD

MATERIALS

- Heavy paper, such as construction paper, or cardboard.
- Embellishments as desired.
- Transfer letters or letters in various sizes cut from magazines, optional.
- Mat knife; pencil with #2 lead; ruler with metal edge.
- Paper cement or hot glue gun and glue sticks, for securing embellishments.

1 Standard place card. Cut 3½" (9 cm) square of heavy paper, using mat knife; mark line through the center, using #2 lead pencil. Score, but do not cut through, the paper on marked line; fold the card along the scored crease.

Assorted letters *in various sizes and colors are cut from a magazine for a whimsical effect.*

Gold stars *(left) in several sizes are scattered on this place card. A large star at the top forms an extended design.*

Dried flowers *(right) accent a place card of handmade paper.*

2 Mark light pencil line on card, about ⅛" (3 mm) below the desired placement for name. Position transfer sheet over card, aligning guideline under desired letter with the pencil line on card; press over letter with wooden stick or pencil. Place lightweight paper over transferred name; rub over letters, to ensure that they are secure.

Place card with extended design. Cut 3½" (9 cm) square of heavy paper, using mat knife; mark line through center, using #2 lead pencil. Transfer or glue the design onto card, with portion of design extending above marked line. Cut out portion of design that extends above line. Score card on both sides of design; do not score across design area. Fold card along scored crease.

Pillows, Pillows, Pillows

DECORATOR PILLOWS

Pillows are an excellent way to add accent colors or unusual textures to your living room decorating scheme. Nestled on sofas and armchairs, pillows help create a warm, inviting atmosphere.

In traditional rooms, pillows are an inexpensive way to use lavish fabrics and trims for a touch of elegance and sophistication. In contemporary rooms, colorful pillows can liven up neutral or solid-colored upholstery pieces.

Knife-edge pillows are quick to make; a simple stitched closure allows the pillow to be decorative on both sides. If desired, emphasize the edges of the pillow by attaching a fringe; most fringes have a decorative heading and may be hand-stitched in place. Another way to trim a pillow is by inserting a twisted welting into the seam at the edges of the pillow.

A variety of other trims, such as braid and gimp, may be applied to the front of a decorator pillow. These trims may be topstitched onto the pillow front before the pillow is assembled.

Pillow forms with polyester fiberfill or down filling are available in a variety of sizes. You may also make your own pillow form, sewing the liner as you would a knife-edge pillow and filling it with polyester fiberfill.

MATERIALS

- Decorator fabric.
- Pillow form.
- Polyester fiberfill, for filling out corners.
- Decorative trim, such as twisted welting or fringe, optional.

HOW TO MAKE A BASIC KNIFE-EDGE PILLOW

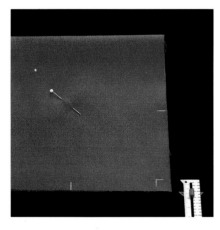

1 Cut pillow front and pillow back 1" (2.5 cm) wider and longer than the pillow form. Fold the pillow front into fourths. Mark a point halfway between corner and fold on each open side. At the corner, mark a point ½" (1.3 cm) from each raw edge.

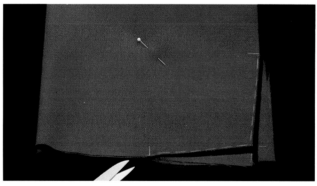

2 Mark lines, tapering from raw edges at center marks to marks at corner. Cut on marked lines.

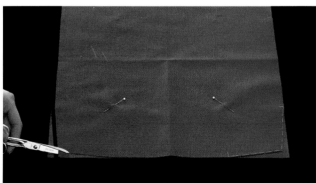

3 Use pillow front as pattern for cutting pillow back so all corners are tapered. This will eliminate dog-eared corners on the finished pillow.

4 Pin pillow front to pillow back, right sides together. Stitch ½" (1.3 cm) seam, leaving opening on one side for turning and for inserting pillow form.

(Continued)

5 Turn pillow cover right side out, pulling out the corners. Press under seam allowances at opening.

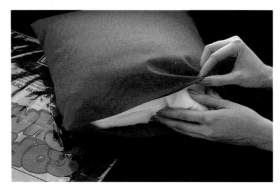

6 Insert pillow form; push fiberfill into the corners of the pillow as necessary to fill out pillow.

7 Pin opening closed; slipstitch or edgestitch close to folded edge.

HOW TO ATTACH TRIMS

Trim without decorative heading. Machine-baste trim to right side of pillow front, with heading of fringe within seam allowance. At ends, cut fringe between loops and hand-stitch loop to secure it; butt ends together. Place pillow front and pillow back right sides together; machine-stitch. Insert pillow form.

Trim with decorative heading. Pin trim around outer edge of pillow cover; miter heading at corners by folding trim at an angle. Hand-stitch along both edges of the trim and along the diagonal fold of mitered corners. Insert pillow form.

HOW TO ATTACH TWISTED WELTING

1 Identify right side of twisted welting; from right side, inner edge of tape is not visible. Stitch twisted welting to *pillow back*, using zipper foot, with right sides up and outer edge of welting tape aligned to raw edge of fabric. Leave 1½" (3.8 cm) unstitched between the ends; leave 3" (7.5 cm) tails.

2 Remove stitching from welting tape on tails. Separate the cords; wrap transparent tape around ends to prevent raveling. Trim ends of the welting tape to 1" (2.5 cm) from stitching; overlap the ends, and secure with transparent tape. Arrange cords so those at right turn up and those at left turn down.

3 Insert cords at right end under the welting tape, twisting them and pulling them down until the welting is returned to its original shape. Secure in place, using tape or pins.

4 Twist and pull cords at left end over cords at right end until the twisted ends look like continuous twisted welting; check both sides of the welting.

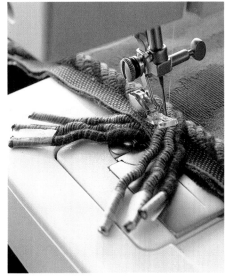

5 Position zipper foot on left side of needle; this will allow you to stitch in the direction of the twists. Machine-baste through all layers to secure the welting at the seamline. Cords may be hand-basted in place, if desired.

6 Place pillow back on pillow front, right sides together. Stitch as close to welting as possible, using zipper foot; leave opening for turning. With pillow front facing up, stitch again, crowding stitches closer to welting.

MORE IDEAS FOR DECORATOR PILLOWS

Banded inset *is the focal point of the velveteen pillow shown above. For added detail, twisted welting edges the pillow; and tassels adorn the corners.*

Decorative cording, *cinched and tied around the simple knife-edge pillows at left, adds detailing. The ends of the cording are finished with end caps.*

Decorative panels *enhance the pillows below. One pillow features a center fabric panel accented with antique lace and buttons; another has a purchased tapestry panel. Gimp, topstitched over the edges, frames the panels.*

Long, twisted fringe drapes gracefully along the sides of the rectangular pillow above.

Strips of leather lacing, woven together, are inserted into the seams at one corner of the pillow at left. Beads, woven in randomly, add color.

Luxurious tassels add an elegant touch to the corners of simple pillows.

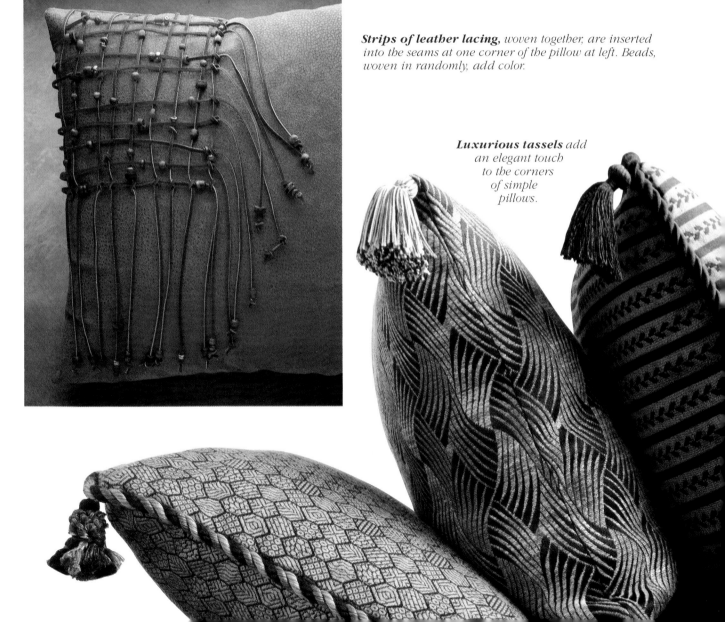

BUTTONED PILLOWS

These easy-to-sew decorative pillows get added style from their interesting buttons. The buttoned envelope-style pillow is sewn from one rectangle and can be made either with a flange (middle) or without (left). The buttoned closure is centered on the pillow, horizontally or vertically.

The buttoned-end pillow (right) is made from two fabric rectangles and features buttoned flanges on both ends of the pillow. Buttons are also sewn to the back side of the flange to make the pillow attractive on both sides.

The fabric yardage requirements vary with the size of the pillow. It may be possible to cut the pillow rectangles on the crosswise grain, depending on the size of the rectangles and on the width and design of the fabric. Decorative shank buttons up to 1¼" (3.2 cm) in diameter are recommended for the buttoned pillows.

HOW TO SEW A BUTTONED ENVELOPE-STYLE PILLOW

MATERIALS

- Decorator fabric.
- Decorative buttons.
- Pillow form.
- Polyester fiberfill.

CUTTING DIRECTIONS

For a horizontal closure, cut one rectangle from fabric, with the length equal to two times the length of the pillow form plus 10" (25.5 cm) for the hems and overlap; for a flanged pillow, also add 8" (20.5 cm) for the flanges. The width of the rectangle is equal to the width of the pillow form plus 1" (2.5 cm) for seam allowances; for a flanged pillow, also add 4" (10 cm) for the flanges.

For a vertical closure, cut one rectangle from fabric, with the length equal to the length of the pillow form plus 1" (2.5 cm) for seam allowances; for a flanged pillow, also add 4" (10 cm) for the flanges. The width of the rectangle is equal to two times the width of the pillow form plus 10" (25.5 cm) for the hems and overlap; for a flanged pillow, also add 8" (20.5 cm) for the flanges.

1 Without flanges. Press under 2" (5 cm) twice to make double-fold hems on both ends of the rectangle, for the closure. Hand-stitch or machine-stitch in place.

2 Make the buttonholes on hem overlap as shown; space the buttonholes evenly between seam allowances and position them about 5⁄8" (1.5 cm) from folded edge.

3 Fold the fabric, right sides together, centering the double-fold hems; place the hem underlap for the buttons on top of hem overlap with buttonholes. Pin, matching the raw edges.

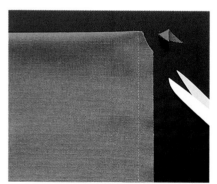

4 Stitch along the raw edges, using 1⁄2" (1.3 cm) seam allowances. Clip the corners diagonally. Turn pillow cover right side out; press.

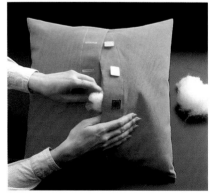

5 Stitch buttons on hem underlap. Insert pillow form; push polyester fiberfill into corners of pillow cover as necessary to fill out pillow. Button the pillow cover.

1 With flanges. Follow steps 1 to 4; in step 2, take into account a 2" (5 cm) flange depth and 1⁄2" (1.3 cm) seam allowances when determining the spacing between the buttonholes. Measure 2" (5 cm) from the edges of pillow cover to mark depth of flange on each side.

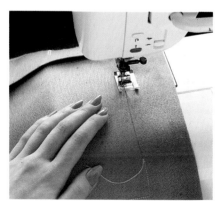

2 Pin layers together. Stitch on the marked lines, pivoting at corners to form the flange. Complete pillow as in step 5.

150

HOW TO SEW A BUTTONED-END PILLOW

MATERIALS

- Decorator fabric.
- Decorative buttons, two for each buttonhole.
- Pillow form.
- Polyester fiberfill.

CUTTING DIRECTIONS

Cut two rectangles from fabric, for the front and the back of the pillow, with the width of the rectangles on the crosswise grain. The width of the fabric rectangles is equal to the longest dimension of the pillow form plus 10" (25.5 cm) for the flanges and facings. The length of the fabric rectangles is equal to the shortest dimension of the pillow form plus 1" (2.5 cm) for seam allowances.

1 Place pillow front and pillow back right sides together. Stitch ½" (1.3 cm) seam on upper and lower edges; leave opening, centered on the lower edge, for inserting the pillow form. Press the seam allowances open.

2 Turn pillow cover right side out. Fold under 3" (7.5 cm) at ends; press lightly.

3 Align the folded edges at ends; pin. Stitch through all layers 2" (5 cm) from folded edges, to form flanges.

4 Mark desired placement for buttonholes; space evenly and center the width of the buttonholes on flanges as shown. Stitch buttonholes through all layers; cut open.

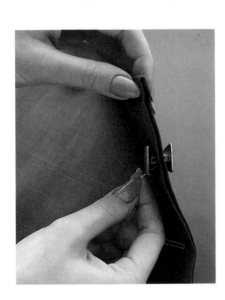

5 Hand-stitch two buttons together so the buttons face in opposite directions; do not cut thread. Insert buttons through a buttonhole so one button is exposed on each side of the flange; tack the buttons in place to prevent any shifting. Repeat for remaining buttons.

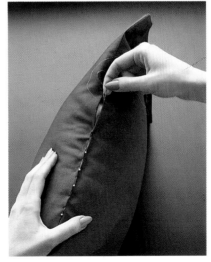

6 Insert pillow form; push polyester fiberfill into corners of pillow cover as necessary to fill out pillow. Pin opening closed, and slipstitch or edgestitch close to folded edge.

TIE-TAB PILLOWS

Tie-tab pillows are created by covering a knife-edge inner pillow with a pillowcase that has a tie-tab closure on one side. The tabs on the case can be tied in knots or bows, depending on the look desired. This pillow style provides an opportunity to combine coordinating fabrics, because the inner pillow is visible between the tie tabs along the closure side.

The number of tabs needed will vary with the size of the pillow. Two tabs are needed for each tie. Evenly space the tabs about 3" to 4" (7.5 to 10 cm) apart.

The instructions that follow are for a knife-edge inner pillow and a tie-tab pillowcase with tapered corners. Tapering the stitching at the corners eliminates dog-eared corners on the finished pillow. If you are making the inner pillow or the pillowcase from a plaid or striped fabric, you may prefer not to taper the corners.

MATERIALS

- Decorator fabric, for inner pillow, pillowcase, and tabs.
- Pillow form.
- Polyester fiberfill, for filling out corners.

CUTTING DIRECTIONS

For the knife-edge inner pillow, cut the pillow front and back 1" (2.5 cm) wider and longer than the pillow form.

For the pillowcase, cut the case front and back 1" (2.5 cm) wider and ½" (1.3 cm) longer than the pillow form. Also cut a facing strip 1½" (3.8 cm) wide, with the length equal to two times the width of the pillow form plus 1" (2.5 cm). For each tab, cut two 1¼" (3.2 cm) strips of fabric. For knotted tabs, cut the strips 8" (20.5 cm) long; for tabs tied into bows, cut the strips 12" (30.5 cm) long.

HOW TO SEW A KNIFE-EDGE PILLOW

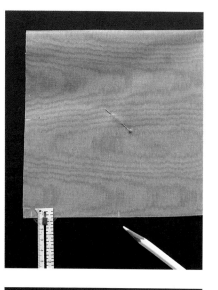

1 Fold pillow front into fourths. For tapered corners, mark a point halfway between corner and fold on each open side. At corner, mark a point ⅜" (1 cm) from each raw edge.

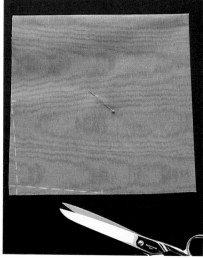

2 Mark lines, tapering from the raw edges at center marks to marks at corner. Cut along the marked lines.

3 Use pillow front as a pattern for cutting pillow back so that all corners are tapered. This will eliminate dog-eared corners on the finished pillow.

4 Pin the pillow front to pillow back, right sides together. Stitch a ½" (1.3 cm) seam, leaving opening on one side for turning and for inserting pillow form.

5 Turn pillow cover right side out, pulling out corners. Press under seam allowances at opening.

6 Insert pillow form; push fiberfill into the corners of the pillow as necessary to fill out pillow.

7 Pin opening closed; slipstitch or edgestitch close to folded edge.

HOW TO SEW A TIE-TAB PILLOWCASE

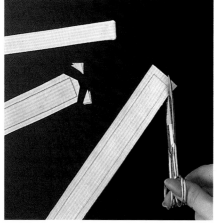

1 Fold pillowcase front in half. Mark and cut tapered corners at one end as in steps 1 and 2, opposite; do not taper corners at edge of case where the ties will be stitched. Use case front as a pattern for case back.

2 Pin case front to case back, right sides together. Stitch around sides, using a ½" (1.3 cm) seam allowance and leaving untapered edge unstitched; press seams open. Turn the case right side out, pulling out the corners.

3 Place two tab strips right sides together, matching the raw edges. Stitch ¼" (6 mm) seam around long sides and one end of tab. Repeat for remaining tabs. Trim corners, and turn the tabs right side out; press.

4 Pin tabs to right side of the case along unstitched edge, keeping the raw edges even and spacing the tabs evenly; position end tabs about 2½" (6.5 cm) from the seam.

5 Fold facing strip, right sides together, matching short ends; stitch ½" (1.3 cm) seam. Press the seam open. Press up ¼" (6 mm) along one edge of the facing strip.

6 Pin unpressed edge of facing strip to open edge of pillowcase, right sides together and raw edges even. Stitch ½" (1.3 cm) seam; trim the seam allowance. Press facing to the wrong side of the case.

7 Machine-stitch or hand-stitch facing in place. Insert pillow. Tie tabs into bows or knots.

MORE IDEAS
FOR PILLOWS

Buttoned envelope-style pillow (page 149) has the overlap positioned near one side of the pillow for an asymmetrical look.

Buttoned-end and tasseled pillows are grouped together for impact. A variety of buttons are used on the buttoned-end pillow (page 149) to give a whimsical look. Ball tassels embellish the corners of the simple knife-edge pillows (page 153).

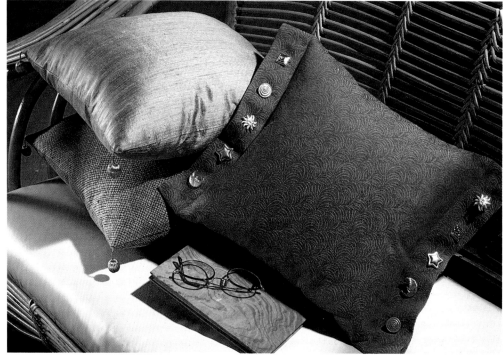

Tapestry pillow is framed with mitered border. The border is applied to the center panel.

Tufted pillow with welting showcases a large center button, which is applied as on page 253.

Southwestern-style pillows are decorated with conchos and beads. Conchos with knotted leather strips are secured to the corners and center of a knife-edge pillow (page 153). Leather laces replace the fabric tabs on a tie-tab pillow (page 153).

Double-flange pillows have an understated look and exceptional versatility. Made from brocades and tapestries, they are elegant in a traditional setting, yet their streamlined design makes them equally elegant in contemporary prints and solids. Select floral prints of polished cotton, and these pillows are right at home in a country room. For these pillows, two mitered panels are stitched together along the inner edge of the border, creating a double flange. At the center of the pillow, a matching or contrasting fabric is tucked under the flange before the pillow front and pillow back are joined.

HOW TO SEW A DOUBLE-FLANGE PILLOW WITH AN INSERT

MATERIALS

- Fabric for pillow front and pillow back, including flange, yardage depending on size of project; for 14" (35.5 cm) pillow form and 2½" (6.5 cm) flange, you will need ¾ yd. (0.7 m) of 54" (137 cm) fabric.
- Fabric for insert at center of pillow; yardage depending on size of project; for 14" (35.5 cm) pillow form, you will need ⅝ yd. (0.6 m).
- Pillow form in desired size.
- Polyester fiberfill, for filling out corners.

CUTTING DIRECTIONS

The size of the inner portion of the pillow is equal to the size of the pillow form. To this measurement, add four times the desired width of the flange plus ½" (1.3 cm) for turning under the raw edges; cut two pieces of fabric this size, for the pillow front and pillow back. For example, for a 14" (35.5 cm) square pillow with a 2½" (6.5 cm) flange, use a 14" (35.5 cm) pillow form, and cut two pieces, each 24½" (62.3 cm) square. For the center insert, add twice the desired depth of the flange to the size of the pillow form; cut one piece of insert fabric.

1 Stitch scant ¼" (6 mm) from edges of pillow front. Fold edges to the wrong side; press just beyond the stitching line. On each side, press under desired depth of flange.

2 Open out the corner; fold diagonally so pressed folds match (arrows). Press diagonal fold.

3 Open out the corner. Fold through center of corner, right sides together. Stitch on diagonal foldline from step 2. Trim fabric at corner ¼" (6 mm) from stitching. Press seam open.

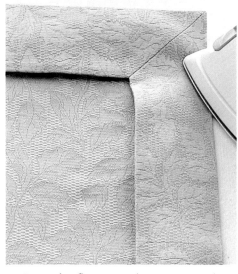

4 Press the flange in place, turning the corners right side out.

5 Place insert fabric on pillow front, tucking raw edges under flange; smooth, and pin in place.

6 Press under sides of pillow back, an amount equal to depth of flange plus ¼" (6 mm), so fabric on folded flange is right side up. Miter corners as in steps 2 to 4.

7 Place pillow front on pillow back, with mitered sides up, matching edges; pin.

8 Stitch around inner edge of flange, securing the insert; pivot at corners, and leave opening on one side for inserting pillow form.

9 Insert the pillow form; push fiberfill into the corners of the pillow as necessary to fill out pillow. Pin the opening closed; complete stitching on inner edge of flange.

MORE IDEAS FOR DOUBLE-FLANGE PILLOWS

Braid trim *(page 164), like the wide, elegant braid on this pillow, adds definition to the inner edge of the flange. The trim is mitered at the corners for a professional finish.*

The simple design of a double-flange pillow lends itself to a number of variations. For additional impact, embellish the pillows with decorative trims. Weave ribbon trims together for an elegant checked effect, or apply them diagonally across the pillow front, creating a free-form pattern. For a different look, trim the inner edge of the flanges with a decorative braid trim.

The center portion of the pillow can have a pieced fabric insert for added interest. Select several coordinating fabrics, piecing them together in either a planned or random design.

Pieced insert *(page 165) can be sewn in either a planned design or in a random, patchwork design.*

Woven insert *made from iridescent ribbons adds impact to a double-flange pillow.*

Diagonal trims *(page 164) are positioned randomly for a creative effect. The printed fabrics used for these pillows reverse to solid black on the wrong side, making the contrasting flanges.*

HOW TO SEW A DOUBLE-FLANGE PILLOW WITH A WOVEN INSERT

MATERIALS

- Fabric for pillow front and pillow back, including flange, yardage depending on size of project; for 14" (35.5 cm) pillow form and 2½" (6.5 cm) flange, you will need ¾ yd. (0.7 m) of 54" (137 cm) fabric.
- Trims, such as ribbons or braids.
- Pillow form in desired size.
- Polyester fiberfill, for filling out corners.

CUTTING DIRECTIONS

Cut pillow front and pillow back as on page 160.

Cut trims 1" (2.5 cm) longer than measurement of pillow form; this allows sufficient length for ¼" (6 mm) seam allowances and for weaving the trims.

1 Follow steps 1 to 4 on page 160. Plan the placement of trims. Apply glue stick to ¼" (6 mm) seam allowance at one end of each vertical trim; secure to pillow front, tucking seam allowance under flange. If necessary, trims may be spaced slightly apart.

2 Secure horizontal trims to pillow front as for vertical trims in step 1. Weave trims together; secure remaining ends of trims under flange, trimming any excess length to ¼" (6 mm) seam allowances. Complete pillow as on page 161, steps 6 to 9.

HOW TO SEW A DOUBLE-FLANGE PILLOW WITH DIAGONAL TRIM

MATERIALS

- Solid-color or reversible fabric for the pillow front and pillow back, including the flange, yardage depending on size of project; for 14" (35.5 cm) pillow form and 2½" (6.5 cm) flange, you will need ¾ yd. (0.7 m) of 54" (137 cm) fabric.
- Trims, such as ribbons.
- Pillow form in desired size.
- Polyester fiberfill, for filling out corners.

CUTTING DIRECTIONS

Cut pillow front and pillow back as on page 160.

1 Follow steps 1 to 4 on page 160. Plan the placement of trims. Cut the trims to the lengths needed, allowing ¼" (6 mm) seam allowances.

2 Secure trims to pillow front with glue stick, tucking raw edges under flange. Stitch in place along edges of the trims. Complete pillow as on page 161, steps 6 to 9.

HOW TO SEW A DOUBLE-FLANGE PILLOW WITH BRAID TRIM

MATERIALS

- Fabric for pillow front and pillow back, including flange, yardage depending on size of project; for 14" (35.5 cm) pillow form and 2½" (6.5 cm) flange, you will need ¾ yd. (0.7 m) of 54" (137 cm) fabric.

- Decorative trim, such as braid, for the inner edge of flange, length equal to perimeter of pillow form plus 2" (5 cm).
- Pillow form in desired size.
- Polyester fiberfill, for filling out corners.

CUTTING DIRECTIONS

Cut pillow front and pillow back as on page 160.

1 Press flange and miter corners on *both* pillow front and pillow back as on page 161, step 6. Mark finished width of flange on unmitered side of pillow front, using chalk.

2 Pin braid to pillow front, with outer edge of braid along marked lines; miter braid at corners by folding it at an angle. Fold end of braid diagonally at final corner; trim excess. Edgestitch along inner edge of braid.

3 Pin pillow front and pillow back together with mitered sides facing. Edgestitch along outer edge of braid, leaving an opening for inserting pillow form; hand-stitch mitered corners in place.

4 Insert the pillow form; push fiberfill into the corners of the pillow as necessary to fill out the pillow. Pin the opening closed; complete stitching on outer edge of braid.

HOW TO SEW A DOUBLE-FLANGE PILLOW WITH A PIECED INSERT

MATERIALS

- Fabric for pillow front and pillow back, including flange, yardage depending on size of project; for 14" (35.5 cm) pillow form and 2½" (6.5 cm) flange, you will need ¾ yd. (0.7 m) of 54" (137 cm) fabric.
- Scraps of several fabrics, for pieced insert.
- Pillow form in desired size.
- Polyester fiberfill, of filling out corners.

CUTTING DIRECTIONS

Cut pillow front and pillow back as on page 160.

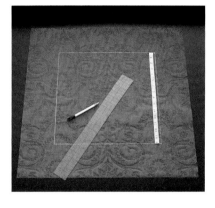

1 Mark square or rectangle, 1" (2.5 cm) larger than pillow form, on wrong side of the pillow front, centering it on the fabric.

2 Cut a patch of fabric, and place in center or corner of marked area; pin in place. Place a second patch on the first patch, right sides together, aligning one edge. Stitch ¼" (6 mm) seam along aligned edges.

3 Flip the second patch right side up; press. Pin in place. Continue to attach patches until marked area is covered.

4 Sew pillow as on pages 160 and 161, omitting step 5.

HABERDASHERY PILLOWS

For a unique accent, create a pillow from men's discarded suits. Nestled among traditional pillows, a haberdashery pillow adds an unexpected touch of whimsy. The instructions opposite are for a trapezoid-shaped pillow about 16" (40.5 cm) high.

Old suits are readily available at secondhand stores or garage sales. Look for jackets with interesting details. Pockets, buttonholes, and manufacturer's labels add interest to the pillow. Do not overlook lining fabrics and lining details. From the suit pants, welted back pockets, portions of the waistband, and the fly front can be used. A necktie may also be used as an accent.

MATERIALS

- Men's suit coat; suit pants or necktie, optional.
- Muslin, for underlining.
- Purchased welting, if desired.
- Lightweight paper, for pattern.
- Polyester fiberfill.

HOW TO MAKE A HABERDASHERY PILLOW

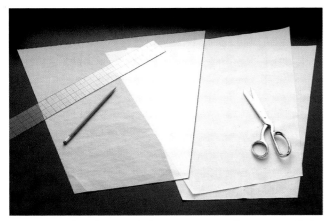

1 Draw 18½" (47.3 cm) line on paper; draw a parallel 9" (23 cm) line centered 17" (43 cm) below first line. Draw connecting lines to make pattern, which includes ½" (1.3 cm) seam allowances. Cut two underlining pieces from muslin, using pattern.

2 Plan placement of major design details for pillow front, such as lapels and pockets, by placing muslin over the garment; mark garment with chalk, and trace design details onto muslin.

3 Cut design pieces from garment, adding ½" (1.3 cm) seam allowances. Cut pieces from the outer layer of the garment only; this allows you to use the lining details for other areas of pillow.

4 Plan placement of smaller pieces, incorporating details such as lining pockets and garment labels. Cut pieces, adding ½" (1.3 cm) seam allowances.

5 Arrange fabric pieces in desired placement; set aside the lapel piece. Stitch remaining pieces to the underlining, using flip-and-stitch and edgestitch methods on page 168. If desired, smaller pieces may be seamed together into larger units before securing them to the underlining.

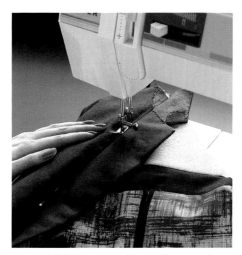

6 Attach lapel piece by stitching under the lapel, about ¼" (6 mm) from the roll line.

(Continued)

7 Repeat steps 2 to 5 on page 167 for pillow back. Baste around outer edges of the pillow front, within ½" (1.3 cm) seam allowances of muslin underlining; repeat for pillow back. From both pieces, trim excess fabric that extends beyond raw edges of the underlining.

8 Baste welting, if desired, to the pillow front, along one or more seams; tape ends of welting into seam allowance.

9 Pin pillow front to pillow back, right sides together. Stitch ½" (1.3 cm) seam around pillow, leaving opening on one side for turning.

10 Turn pillow right side out, pulling out corners. Press under seam allowances of opening. Stuff the pillow with fiberfill. Slipstitch or edgestitch opening closed.

TIPS FOR JOINING DESIGN PIECES

1 **Stitch-and-flip method.** Apply any garment pieces that have raw edges by placing one piece on muslin underlining; pin in place. Place a second piece on the first piece, right sides together, aligning raw edges. Stitch ½" (1.3 cm) from aligned edges.

2 Flip top garment piece right side up; press. Pin in place. Continue attaching pieces, pressing under ½" (1.3 cm) seam allowance on any raw edges that will not be covered by another piece.

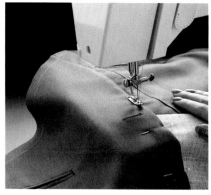

Edgestitch method. Apply any pieces that have finished edges, such as the garment front edge, by stitching them to the muslin underlining close to the finished edge of each piece.

Men's shirt *is used for the haberdashery pillow, above left, with a necktie added for an accent of color. Men's suit trousers are used for the rectangular pillow, above right. Details include the welted back pocket, the fly front, and the pants cuffs; suspenders were also added.*

School band uniform, *a memento of school activities, makes a unique haberdashery pillow.*

TWIG BASKETS

Twisted handle *is made from intertwined, small-diameter branches of dogwood. Each branch of the handle is nailed into the basket twigs.*

Perfect for a country setting or an eclectic style, these rustic twig baskets are assembled easily using a simple stacking method of construction. Since the baskets are made from gathered twigs, the only purchased materials are the wire nails.

Gather the twigs from a wooded area, looking for twigs that are straight and have a smooth bark. Willow is popular for twig baskets because its high moisture content makes it flexible and prevents it from splitting, but many other woods may also be used. Select twigs with a diameter of 3/8" to 3/4" (1 to 2 cm), depending on the desired finished size of the basket. You may gather twigs that have fallen to the ground or cut branches from living trees.

If you plan to have a handle on the basket, you will need to cut that branch from a living tree, selecting one that can be bent into the curved shape without cracking. Plan to use the branch soon after it has been cut to prevent it from drying out.

When nailing two twigs together, select a nail that is no longer than the combined diameter of the two twigs. As you stack the twigs to form the sides, you may use a longer nail, because you will be nailing into the twig below as well as into the two being joined. To prevent the small-diameter nails from bending, support the nail with your thumb and forefinger; this is especially important if you are using hardwood twigs. It is also helpful to tap the nail lightly to avoid bending it.

MATERIALS

- Straight twigs with a smooth bark.
- Wire nails or brads in 5/8", 3/4", and 1" (1.5, 2, and 2.5 cm) lengths.
- Hand saw; pruning shears; tack hammer.

Basket with dividers *organizes and displays kitchen items. The twig dividers were stacked, row by row, as the basket sides were assembled.*

HOW TO MAKE A TWIG BASKET

1 Cut twigs to the desired lengths. Lay two twigs on the work surface parallel to each other. Lay two more twigs on top of and perpendicular to the first two; overlap the twigs about 1" (2.5 cm) at corners.

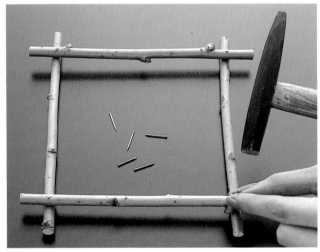

2 Nail the twigs together at intersecting corners, using nails of appropriate length.

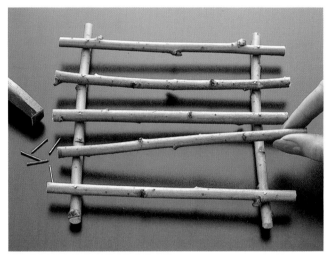

3 Lay twigs for the bottom of the basket perpendicular to first two twigs, spacing them about 1¼" to 1½" (3.2 to 3.8 cm) apart. Nail in place.

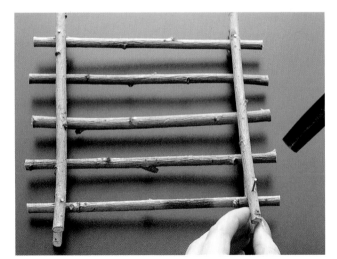

4 Lay two twigs perpendicular to the last row of twigs to begin building the sides of the basket. Nail in place at intersections, using 1" (2.5 cm) nails.

5 Add twigs, two at a time, laying them perpendicular to each previous row; nail in place, using 1" (2.5 cm) nails. Continue until the desired height is reached.

HOW TO ADD A HANDLE TO A TWIG BASKET

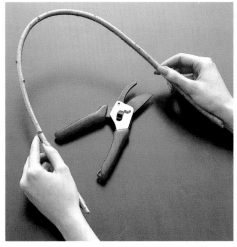

1 Cut branch to desired length for handle. Bend the branch to determine in which direction it bends more easily.

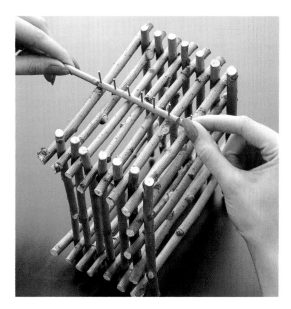

2 Place handle on center of one side of basket, with cut end of branch even with bottom of the basket. Press nails of appropriate length into handle where it intersects twigs of basket.

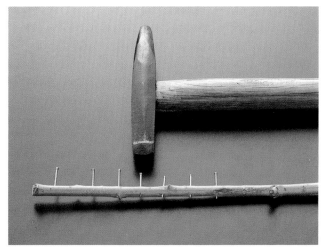

3 Lay handle on sturdy work surface; drive nails through the diameter of the handle.

4 Reposition the handle on the basket; nail in place.

5 Bend the handle to the other side of the basket. Repeat steps 2 to 4.

6 Nail the handle again through each twig (arrow), from the inside of the basket, using side of hammer, if necessary.

MARKET
BASKETS

The distinctive quality of a handmade basket adds a warm, decorative accent to any room. An easy-to-make market basket, sturdy enough to use for generations, can be completed in about three hours. The base, or bottom, of the basket measures about 6" × 10" (15 × 25.5 cm), and the sides are about 4½" (11.5 cm) high. The sturdy, wooden D-handle also doubles as a support for the market basket.

Basket materials are available from many fiber-art stores and craft stores as well as from mail-order suppliers. The reeds are made pliable by soaking them in warm water before weaving; a soaking time of three to five minutes is sufficient for most reeds. Determine the right and wrong sides of flat reeds as on page 178, step 2. When weaving baskets, place the right sides of the reeds to the outside of the basket.

The reeds may be left natural or stained in a wood tone or decorator color. Water-based basket stains or wood stains may be used; stains that contain a sealer add a protective finish to the basket. Solid-colored baskets are stained after the basket is completed. Multicolored baskets like those on pages 182 and 183 can be made by staining the reeds before weaving; test the stain to be sure it will not streak when the reeds are soaked. You may want to make a solid-colored basket, to become familiar with the techniques, before designing and weaving a multicolored basket.

Market basket has a sturdy *D-handle*. Basket construction starts by weaving flat reeds to form the base, or bottom. These flat reeds are then upset, or turned up, to form the *stakes* for the sides of the basket; flat reeds, called *weavers*, are woven between the stakes, forming the sides. Two oval reeds are placed at the upper edge to form the rim; this provides an attractive edge and adds stability. *Sea grass* is inserted at the top of the rim, filling the space between the oval reeds, for a decorative finish. The rim is secured by wrapping it with a narrow oval reed; this reed, and the process of wrapping it, are referred to as *lashing*.

MATERIALS

- 6" × 10" (15 × 25.5 cm) D-handle.
- ⅝" (1.5 cm) flat reed, for stakes and weavers.
- ½" (1.3 cm) flat reed, for weaver.
- ½" (1.3 cm) flat oval reed, for rim.

- Sea grass, for rim filler.
- ¼" (6 mm) flat oval reed, for lashing.
- Reed cutter or utility scissors.
- Awl.

- Clothespins.
- Water-based basket stain or wood stain, optional; paintbrush or sponge applicator, for applying the stain.

1 Cut ⅝" (1.5 cm) flat reed into five 25" (63.5 cm) lengths and eight 21" (53.5 cm) lengths; these will be used to form the base and stakes. Soak strips in warm water for about 3 minutes.

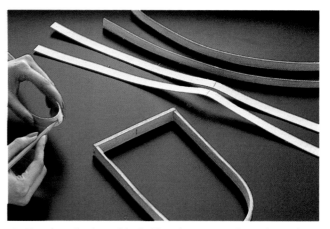

2 Bend soaked reed in half to determine the right and wrong sides; right side remains smooth, while wrong side splinters and appears hairy. Mark the centers of 25" (63.5 cm) reeds on wrong side, using pencil. Mark center of handle bottom on inside.

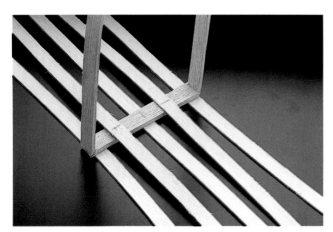

3 Position three marked strips under handle and two strips over handle, with right sides down and center marks at handle. Strips should be evenly spaced, with center strip aligned with center mark on handle and outside strips even with edge of handle.

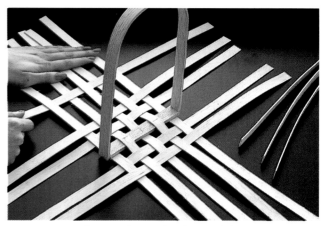

4 Weave 21" (53.5 cm) strip ½" (1.3 cm) from one side of handle, weaving under, over, under, over, and under the base reeds. Repeat with a second strip on opposite side of handle. Continue weaving, alternating sides, until four strips are woven on each side of handle.

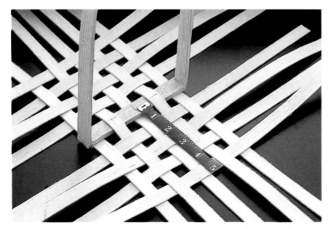

5 Adjust spacing of strips as necessary, so distance from center of handle to outside edge of last woven strip measures 5" (12.5 cm). Base size is 6" × 10" (15 × 25.5 cm).

6 Upset the sides by bending each stake toward the inside of the basket, rewetting reeds, if necessary.

7 Soak coil of ⅝" (1.5 cm) flat reed to be used as weavers. Center the end of reed over outside of first stake before handle; clamp with clothespin. Weave strip under handle and continue weaving to first corner.

8 Pinch reed gently at the corner to shape basket. Continue weaving to starting point; clamp as necessary.

9 Cut reed even with center of the second stake beyond handle.

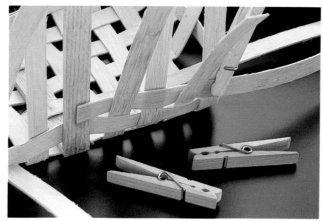

10 Weave over the starting end of the weaver, then under handle; the cut end of the weaver will be concealed by the stake after it is upset.

11 Turn basket around to opposite side; weave second row, beginning in center of handle and weaving under first stake. At end, cut reed even with third stake beyond handle and weave over the starting end; then finish weaving the reed.

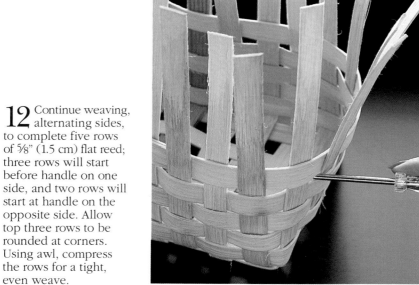

12 Continue weaving, alternating sides, to complete five rows of ⅝" (1.5 cm) flat reed; three rows will start before handle on one side, and two rows will start at handle on the opposite side. Allow top three rows to be rounded at corners. Using awl, compress the rows for a tight, even weave.

13 Cut strip of ½" (1.3 cm) flat reed to measurement around top of basket plus 4" (10 cm); soak. Weave a sixth row, starting at center of handle.

(Continued)

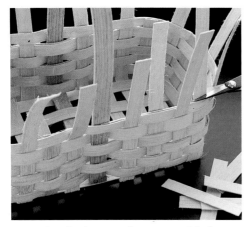

14 Cut the inner stakes even with the upper edge of the reed.

15 Bend outer stakes to the inside, rewetting them as necessary. Trim stakes at an angle; tuck them under the weaver, third row from the top, concealing pointed end.

16 Cut two strips of ½" (1.3 cm) flat oval reed to the measurement around the top of the basket plus 4" (10 cm); soak. Beginning about 1" (2.5 cm) before handle (arrow), wrap the reed around outside of the basket, with flat side of reed against top row of weaving; clamp with clothespins. Trim reed at an angle, at center of handle; the cut edge will be concealed with the lashing.

17 Position remaining strip of flat oval reed on inside of basket, against top row of weaving, overlapping ends at the opposite side of basket.

18 Cut one strip of sea grass and position it between the reeds at top of basket on one side. Repeat for other side.

19 Cut a strip of ¼" (6 mm) flat oval reed about 90" (229 cm) long, to be used for lashing; soak. Starting on side where inner rim overlaps, tuck end of lashing under lower edge of inner rim.

20 Insert lashing under rim, between the handle and stake, passing it from inside of basket to outside; if necessary, use awl to separate reeds so lashing can be inserted. Pull the lashing snug.

21 Wrap the lashing up and over rim and through next space between stakes; continue lashing around the basket to handle on opposite side.

22 Bring the lashing diagonally across the handle on outside of basket; from inside of basket, insert the lashing under rim directly below the place where the lashing crosses the top of the rim.

23 Bring the lashing diagonally across handle on the outside and inside; reinsert the lashing through the previous space to outside of basket.

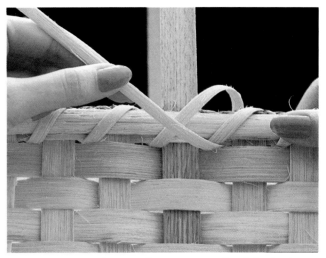

24 Continue lashing to the opposite side of the basket; make an X over handle on outside of basket.

25 Cut lashing at an angle, and tuck the cut end under weaver below handle on inside of basket.

26 Allow basket to dry thoroughly. Trim loose hairs. Apply stain to basket, if desired; stain may be thinned with water, if necessary.

MORE IDEAS FOR MARKET BASKETS

Stained weavers *contrast with the stakes, creating a simple, yet colorful, design.*

Weavers in graduated widths *are used for this stained basket. Starting at the base of stakes, weave five rows of ¼" (6 mm) flat reed, three rows of ½" (1.3 cm) reed, and one row of ⅝" (1.5 cm) reed before adding the rim.*

Sea grass, *woven between ½" (1.3 cm) weavers, adds texture. Soak the sea grass before weaving. Because the sea grass is too heavy to overlap, begin and end the weaving inside the basket, allowing the ends to extend.*

Center band is composed of a ⁵⁄₈" (1.5 cm) reed in dark blue, bordered by ¼" (6 mm) natural reeds. Natural sea grass edges the top of the basket, and the remaining reeds, stained light blue, are ½" (1.3 cm) wide.

Larger basket is made using an 8"× 12" (20.5 × 30.5 cm) D-handle and has a woven base of 8"× 12" (20.5 × 30.5 cm). From ⁵⁄₈" (1.5 cm) flat reed, cut seven 32" (81.5 cm) lengths and ten 28" (71 cm) lengths for the base and stakes. For the weavers, cut seven 46" (117 cm) lengths.

Contrasting rim and weavers accent this market basket. Starting at the base of the stakes, weave two rows of ⁵⁄₈" (1.5 cm) flat reed, three rows of ¼" (6 mm) reed, and two rows of ⁵⁄₈" (1.5 cm) reed before adding the rim.

DECORATING
BASKETS

Add your personal touch to purchased baskets by topping them lavishly with ivy or garland, then adding embellishments, such as latex fruit or silk flowers.

For a more rustic look, encircle a basket with bundles of wheat, and tie it with raffia. Or trim the rim of the basket with moss, fallen birch bark, and other dried naturals. For a romantic touch, simply weave a fancy ribbon into an open-weave basket.

Baskets with lids can be made into decorative accessories that provide hidden storage space. Top the lid with silk flowers or preserved leaves. Or embellish the lid with items that reflect a hobby, such as beach-combed seashells, sewing notions, or fishing tackle.

Most items can be secured to baskets using a hot glue gun and glue sticks. For temporary placement, you can secure items with wire or floral adhesive clay.

Moss trims the rim of a basket, with a fanciful bird's nest used as an accent.

Ivy tops this birch basket and twists around the handle. The clusters of latex berries complete the arrangement.

Woven ribbon adds a simple but elegant touch to an open-weave metal basket.

Dried naturals, including pods and preserved leaves, add interest to the lid of the basket at right.

Wheat stems, bundled together, encircle a basket (opposite). Raffia adds a touch of country.

HOW TO MAKE AN IVY-TOPPED BASKET

MATERIALS

- Basket.
- Silk ivy vines or artificial garland.
- Embellishments, such as latex fruit or silk flowers.
- Wire and wire cutter; or hot glue gun and glue sticks.

1 Cut several vines of ivy or a length of artificial garland, and arrange around top of basket; secure with wire or hot glue.

2 Twist ivy around handle of basket, if desired; secure with wire or hot glue. Arrange and secure latex fruit or silk flowers.

HOW TO MAKE A WHEAT-STEM BASKET

MATERIALS

- Wheat with long stems.
- Rubber bands.
- Raffia.
- Old scissors.
- Hot glue gun and glue sticks.

1 Cut several wheat stems to desired lengths, using old scissors. Group stems in bundles; secure with rubber bands.

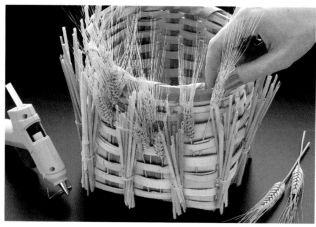 

2 Secure bundles to sides of basket, using hot glue. Add heads of wheat, tucking stem ends into or between the bundles.

3 Tie a length of raffia around the basket, concealing rubber bands.

HOW TO MAKE A MOSS-RIMMED BASKET

MATERIALS

- Moss.
- Embellishments, such as lichens, fallen birch bark, twigs, and other dried naturals; small craft bird's nest, optional.
- Hot glue gun and glue sticks.

1 Secure pieces of moss to basket rim, using hot glue, applying it to both the inside and the outside of rim.

2 Glue lichens and other dried naturals to moss, scattering them around the rim. Glue bird's nest in place, if desired.

HOW TO EMBELLISH A BASKET WITH WOVEN RIBBON

MATERIALS

- Open-weave basket.
- Ribbon and bow.
- Large-eyed needle.
- Wire, for securing bow.

1 Thread ribbon into a large-eyed needle. Weave ribbon in and out of the basket.

2 Wire bow to one side of basket, concealing ends of woven ribbon.

HOW TO EMBELLISH A BASKET WITH A LID

MATERIALS

- Basket with lid.
- Embellishments, such as dried seed pods, stones, and preserved leaves.
- Hot glue gun and glue sticks.

1 Arrange dominant or larger embellishments on lid of basket as desired. Secure with hot glue. Some items can be used as a base for smaller items to add height to the arrangement.

2 Add secondary or smaller embellishments, stacking items as desired.

Rag baskets are simple to construct and can be made in many sizes, from tabletop baskets to large floor baskets. Large baskets with lids can be used to store items such as toys, linens, and seasonal clothing. The baskets are made by wrapping narrow strips of fabric around basket cording as it is coiled into shape. Wooden handles may be added at the sides, or handles may be shaped from the cording.

The basket cording is available in ½" or ¾" (1.3 or 2 cm) diameter at craft and quilting shops as well as through mail-order suppliers. Use the narrow cording for small baskets and the wider cording for large floor baskets.

Traditionally made from leftover fabrics, rag baskets can also be made from discarded clothing, bed sheets, or newly purchased fabrics. Depending on the look you want to achieve, use the same fabric throughout the entire basket or combine several fabrics.

The fabric and cording yardages vary greatly with the size of the baskets. Shown opposite, the basket with the lid is 15" (38 cm) high and 17" (43 cm) in diameter; it requires 11 yd. (10.12 m) fabric and 50 yd. (46 m) of ¾" (2 cm) basket cording. The smaller basket is 10" (25.5 cm) high and 8" (20.5 cm) in diameter; it requires 3½ yd. (3.2 m) fabric and 20 yd. (18.4 m) of ½" (1.3 cm) cording. Approximate yardages are also given for the baskets on pages 192 and 193. To determine the amount of each fabric needed, divide the total yardage by the number of fabrics to be used.

MATERIALS

- Firmly woven, mediumweight fabrics, such as cotton broadcloth.
- Basket cording in ½" (1.3 cm) diameter for small baskets or ¾" (2 cm) diameter for large baskets.
- Tapestry needle, size 13.
- Masking tape or duct tape.
- Rotary cutter and cutting mat.
- Wooden rings, for handles, optional.
- Large wooden bead, for top of lid, optional.

HOW TO MAKE A RAG BASKET

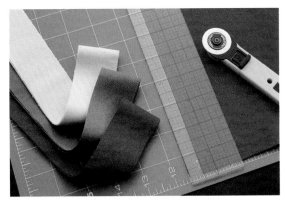

1 Cut fabric on crosswise grain into 1½" (3.8 cm) strips, about 45" (115 cm) long.

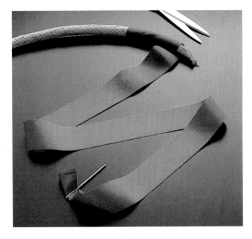

2 Taper end of cording with scissors. Thread fabric strip into a tapestry needle. Beginning about 5" (12.5 cm) from end of cording, wrap unthreaded end of strip tightly around cording, wrapping away from you, almost to end.

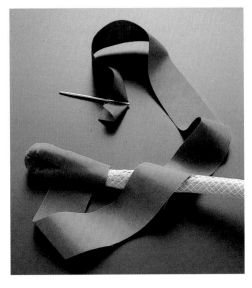

3 Fold end of the cording to make a loop; wrap fabric twice over both cords to secure the loop, leaving small hole. Continue wrapping strip away from you around 3" (7.5 cm) of the uncovered cording, with the uncovered cording to the right.

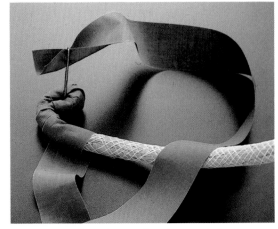

4 Begin coiling the cording into a circle. Secure coil by inserting needle into center hole and pulling fabric through firmly; repeat.

(Continued)

5 Wrap strip around the uncovered cording about three times, wrapping away from you, with the uncovered cording to the right. Secure coil by inserting needle into center hole and pulling fabric firmly; secure coil a second time.

6 Wrap strip around the uncovered cording about three times; splice strips as necessary by lapping new strip over end of previous strip.

7 Secure coil with a joining wrap by inserting needle between rows of previously wrapped cording and pulling the fabric firmly; repeat. If desired, stabilize the joining wrap as in steps 8 and 9; or omit these steps and proceed to step 10.

8 Insert strip between wrapped and unwrapped cords; then bring it up just before the joining wrap (arrow); this will form a loop on the opposite side of the basket.

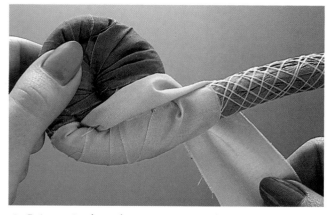

9 Bring strip down between wrapped and unwrapped cords. Continue by wrapping away from you.

10 Splice cording, when necessary, by tapering ends of cords for about 4" (10 cm). Overlap ends, and wrap with masking tape.

11 Wrap and secure the coil until the bottom is desired diameter. Start to build up the sides by laying cording on top of outer row.

12 Construct sides of basket by building up rows of cording. If desired, taper sides by gradually spiraling larger coils. If desired, add handles and knob (opposite).

13 Cut cording at an angle when the basket is desired height; wrap with fabric strip. Secure end of cording to the previous coil by wrapping several times with fabric strip. Conceal end of fabric strip, trimming excess.

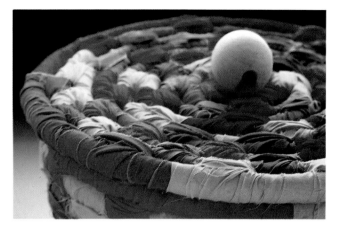

14 Make a lid, if desired, using the same method as for bottom of basket, with diameter of lid slightly larger than basket top. Add wooden knob (below).

HOW TO ADD WOODEN HANDLES & KNOB

Handles. Secure wooden ring to side of basket with a joining wrap, as in step 7; wrap fabric around ring four times for added strength. Continue halfway around basket; attach second handle.

Knob. Thread a fabric strip through a large wooden bead; position at center of lid. Insert ends of fabric strip through lid to underside; knot to secure.

HOW TO ADD FABRIC HANDLES

Handles at top. Secure coil with a joining wrap, as in step 7. Wrap cording for 5" to 6" (12.5 to 15 cm), and shape it to form a handle. Secure with joining wrap. Continue halfway around basket, and make second handle.

Handles at sides. Follow step at left, as for handles at top of basket; then wrap next row until you reach first handle. Secure basket under the handle with a joining wrap that wraps around one or two coils, as shown. Continue the row to the second handle; secure.

MORE IDEAS
FOR RAG BASKETS

Decorative cords and beads *embellish this small basket. This basket measures 5" (12.5 cm) high and is 9" (23 cm) in diameter; it requires about 1 yd. (0.95 m) fabric and 8 yd. (7.35 m) of ½" (1.3 cm) basket cording.*

Floor baskets *add textural interest to a room. The larger basket is 19" (48.5 cm) high and 11" (28 cm) in diameter; it requires 4½ yd. (4.15 m) fabric and 25 yd. (23 m) of ¾" (2 cm) cording. The smaller basket is 9" (23 cm) high and 13" (33 cm) in diameter at the widest point; it requires 3 yd. (2.75 m) fabric and 16 yd. (14.72 m) of ¾" (2 cm) cording.*

Fabric strips *are tied randomly around the joining wraps after the entire basket is coiled. This basket is 5" (12.5 cm) high and 9" (23 cm) in diameter at the base; it requires 1⅝ yd. (1.5 m) fabric and 12 yd. (11.04 m) of ½" (1.3 cm) cording.*

Matching fabric *is used to coordinate a flat basket with the quilt in this bedroom. This basket is 3" (7.5 cm) high and 12" (30.5 cm) in diameter at the top; it requires 1¾ yd. (1.6 m) fabric and 8 yd. (7.35 m) of ½" (1.3 cm) cording.*

Hamper with lid *(right) is 21" (53.5 cm) high and 17" (43 cm) in diameter at the base; it requires 15 yd. (13.8 m) fabric and 64 yd. (58.88 m) of ¾" (2 cm) cording.*

WALL BASKETS

Wall baskets can be filled with dried line and filler materials. Dominant and secondary flowers may also be added, if desired. You may want to embellish the arrangement with a ribbon or raffia bow.

HOW TO MAKE A WALL BASKET

MATERIALS

- Eucalyptus or other line material.
- Dried roses, strawflowers, globe amaranth, and nigella pods or other filler materials.
- Wall basket.
- Floral foam for dried arranging.
- Sheet moss.
- Wire cutter.
- 22-gauge paddle floral wire.

1 Line basket with moss, if necessary. Cut the foam to fit basket. Insert wire through foam, placing small twig between wire and foam; pull wire through foam to back side.

2 Insert foam into basket. Pull wire through back of basket; twist to secure. Cover foam with sheet moss; mist moss lightly with water.

3 Insert sprigs of eucalyptus into foam; fan out evenly.

4 Insert filler materials into arrangement, one variety at a time, spacing evenly.

GARDEN BOXES

In European design, individual elements are grouped in separate areas instead of being mixed throughout the arrangement. European-style floral arrangements resembling miniature gardens fit well into casual living environments; a more formal look can be achieved by using decorative containers of brass or painted ceramic.

Fruits and berries can be interspersed among flowers for visual contrast. Garden boxes can be made with materials of varying heights, placing taller materials in the center or back of the container and shorter materials along the edges. Or use materials of uniform height arranged in geometric patterns, as on page 198.

HOW TO MAKE A GARDEN BOX OF VARYING HEIGHTS

MATERIALS

- Dried larkspur and limonium or other line materials.
- Dried strawflowers, globe amaranth, and lavender or other secondary flowers.
- Preserved leatherleaf or other dried foliage.
- Artificial fruits, such as apples and grapes, on wire or wooden stems.

- Rectangular container.
- Floral foam for dried arranging.
- Sheet moss.
- Wire cutter; serrated knife; scissors.
- Floral pins.

1 Insert floral foam into container, and cover with moss; secure with floral pins. Trim off excess moss with scissors, or tuck excess into sides of container.

2 Fill about one-third of container on left side with larkspur or tallest line material, staying 1½" (3.8 cm) away from edges. Insert limonium about 2" (5 cm) away from larkspur.

3 Insert wired apples between the two line materials, near base. Place grape clusters in front of the larkspur, inserting one slightly higher than the other; allow them to cascade downward.

4 Insert the remaining flowers around line materials, clustering the flowers by variety. Place longer stems near the center and the shorter stems near the outer edges. Stems closest to the center point upward, and stems closer to the outer edges point outward.

5 Insert leatherleaf to fill in any bare areas; intersperse among flowers, if necessary.

HOW TO MAKE A GARDEN BOX OF UNIFORM HEIGHT

MATERIALS

- Dried materials such as miniature artichokes, nigella pods, cockscomb, pomegranates, poppy pods, strawflowers, and garlic bulbs.

- Rectangular container.

- Floral foam for dried arranging.

- Sheet moss.

- Wire cutter; serrated knife.

- String.

- Hot glue gun and glue sticks.

1 Insert foam into the container, and cover. For dried materials with stems, cut the stems 1" to 1½" (2.5 to 3.8 cm) below flower head or pod.

2 Divide container into sections of equal size, using string. Apply hot glue to stems or underside of dried materials; insert a different variety into each section, keeping height of floral materials even.

MORE IDEAS FOR GARDEN BOXES

Thatched box (left) combines lavender, roses, and rye in a parallel design, with equal space devoted to each. Floral materials rise 10" (25 cm) above the rim of the container.

Shadow box is filled with colorful flower heads, arranged in diagonal rows. The flowers are glued to a moss-covered sheet of foam board cut to fit in the shadow box.

Wooden box (right) contains grains, cattails, sunflowers, and poppy pods, arranged in vertical groupings. An array of dried and artificial fruits is inserted near the base.

GARDEN BASKETS

Floor baskets containing potted florals bring a garden look into any interior. Use one as an accent near a fireplace or next to a favorite chair. This versatile basket arrangement also works well in a bedroom or entryway. It is made by placing three clay pots into a large basket, filling them with dried naturals, and surrounding them with moss.

HOW TO MAKE A GARDEN BASKET

MATERIALS

- Dried roses, larkspur, and oregano or other dried materials.
- Basket with handle, about 15" × 18" (38 × 46 cm).
- Three clay pots, about 6" (15 cm) in diameter.
- Floral foam for dried arranging.
- Spanish moss and sheet moss.
- Wire cutter; serrated knife.
- Hot glue gun and glue sticks.

1 Cut thin layer of foam to fit inside bottom of basket. Secure foam to basket, using hot glue. Cover bottoms of pots with hot glue, and press them into foam base, allowing pots to tip outward slightly, if desired.

2 Cut foam into pieces, and wedge into the area between pots and basket, keeping height of foam 2" (5 cm) below top edges of pots. Cover foam with sheet moss, securing it with hot glue. Also insert foam into clay pots, and cover with Spanish moss.

3 Insert one variety of dried natural into each pot, starting at center of pot and working out in a circle until the desired fullness is achieved. Stems in outer rows may be shorter than stems in center. Within a single variety, flowers may be positioned on each side of the handle. Fill in around edges of pots with additional Spanish moss, if desired.

FLOWER BOXES

Boxes filled with an abundance of flowers are a cheerful addition to any kitchen. These flower boxes are fast and easy to construct. The boards are simply butted together and nailed, with strips of corner molding glued in place at the top and corners for a finished look.

The flower boxes can be made in any size. In the instructions that follow, cutting directions are included for a large box that accommodates three 6" (15 cm) clay pots and a small box that accommodates three 4" (10 cm) pots.

The flower boxes may be painted or stained to complement the kitchen decorating scheme. You may choose to finish them using a decorative paint finish.

MATERIALS

- 1 × 8 aspen or maple board, 7 ft. (2.17 m) in length, for large flower box; or 1 × 6 board, 6 ft. (1.85 m) in length, for small flower box.
- 8-ft. (2.48 m) length of 1⅛" (2.8 cm) corner molding for large or small flower box.
- 1¼" 3d finish nails; nail set; wood glue.
- Miter box and backsaw.
- Paint or stain, for desired wood finish.

CUTTING DIRECTIONS

For a large flower box, cut two 7¼" × 22½" (18.7 × 57.3 cm) pieces from 1 × 8 board, for front and back pieces. Also cut two 7¼" × 7¼" (18.7 × 18.7 cm) sides pieces and one 7¼" × 21" (18.7 × 53.5 cm) bottom piece.

For small flower box, cut two 5½" × 16½" (14 × 41.8 cm) pieces from 1 × 6 board, for front and back pieces. Also cut two 5½" × 5½" (14 × 14 cm) side pieces and one 5½" × 15" (14 × 38 cm) bottom piece.

Flower boxes *can be made in various paint finishes. For traditional decorating, the small box above is painted in white enamel. For a country kitchen, the large box opposite has a farmhouse finish; for the lettering, use precut stencils and aerosol paint.*

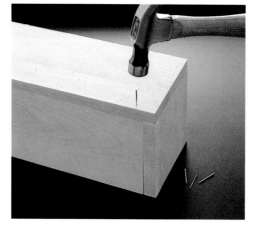

2 Align the bottom piece to the front and side pieces. Drilling through front of box into bottom piece, predrill holes for nails at 4" (10 cm) intervals. Secure with nails.

1 Align one front piece to one side piece as shown. Drilling through front of box into the side piece, predrill two holes for nails about 1" (2.5 cm) deep, using 1/16" drill bit. Secure pieces with nails. Repeat for remaining side piece.

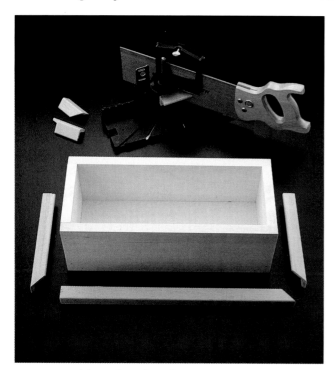

3 Align back piece to the sides and bottom. Drilling through back of box into the side and bottom pieces, predrill holes and secure with nails.

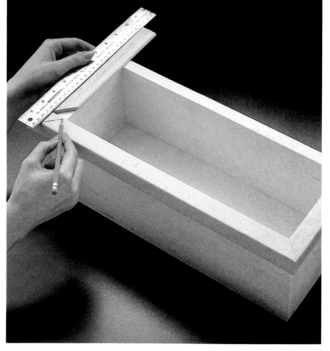

4 Miter moldings for sides of box at front corners; leave excess length on the molding strips. Miter one corner on the molding for front of box, leaving excess length.

5 Position mitered front and side molding strips at one corner. Mark finished length of front piece; mark the angle of the cut. Cut miter.

6 Reposition moldings. Mark finished length and angle of cut for side pieces; miter.

7 Miter one corner on molding for the back of box, leaving excess length. Position with side strip; mark finished length. Cut miter.

8 Reposition moldings; sand the corners, if necessary, for proper fit. Glue moldings around top of box, using wood glue.

9 Measure from lower edge of the molding to the bottom of box; cut pieces to fit all four corners. Sand the cut edges. Glue moldings in place at the corners.

10 Set the nails at the bottom of box, using nail set. Stain or paint flower box as desired, filling the nail holes with paint or with putty to match stain. Apply clear acrylic finish, if desired.

Dress up simple, unfinished wooden boxes with decorative moldings and medallions. Available in a variety of styles, these trims may be glued to the sides of the box and on the lid.

Craft stores that stock miniature supplies have a variety of moldings and medallions for doll houses. These decorative trims are made of soft wood and are easy to work with. Specialty woodworking stores carry cabinetry trims in narrow widths that are also suitable for trimming boxes.

Moldings are easily cut using a miter box and backsaw, or even the small miter box and backsaw intended for use with miniature moldings. Select a backsaw that has a fine-tooth blade.

Many trims may be secured simply by gluing the trims in place and clamping them until dry; place a scrap of lumber or a felt pad under the clamps to protect the wood. For a secure bond and to reduce the need for clamping, you may want to insert brads at the corners of the moldings.

Trims may be stained or painted to match or contrast with the box. If contrasting trims are desired, paint or stain the trims before attaching them to the box.

MATERIALS

- Unfinished wooden box.
- Decorative moldings and medallions.
- Wood glue; emery board or sandpaper.
- Miter box and backsaw.
- Clamps, optional.
- Brads and nail set, optional.
- Stain or paint as desired; wood putty to match stain.

Narrow moldings and small medallions *are available at stores specializing in miniatures and at woodworking stores.*

Wooden boxes, *trimmed with moldings and medallions, can be stained, as shown above, or painted in contrasting colors, as shown opposite.*

HOW TO ADD WOOD TRIMS TO A BOX

1 Miter moldings for sides of box at front corners; leave excess length on the molding strips. Miter one corner on molding for the front of the box, leaving excess length.

2 Position mitered front and side molding strips at one corner. Mark the finished length of the front piece; mark the angle of the cut. Cut miter. Repeat for side piece.

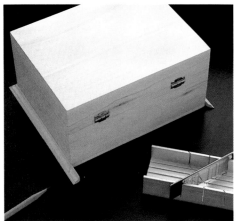

3 Reposition moldings; mark second side piece, and miter to fit.

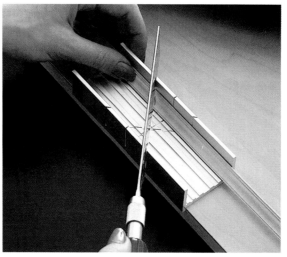

4 Miter one corner on molding for the back of box, leaving excess length. Position with side strip; mark length of opposite corner. Cut miter.

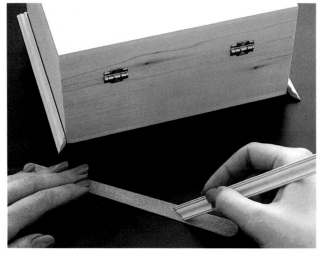

5 Reposition moldings; sand corners, using emery board or sandpaper, as necessary for proper fit.

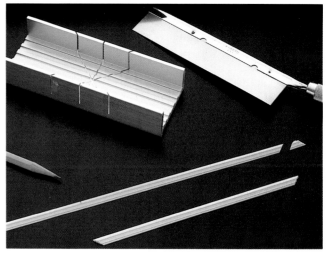

6 Determine outside dimensions for inset frame. Mark one length on the outer edge of molding; cut inside miters at each end. Cut a second strip for opposite side of frame, making sure lengths are even.

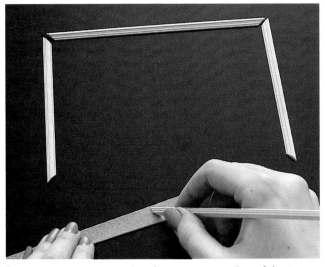

7 Repeat to cut strips that fit remaining sides of the inset frame. Sand corners, using emery board or sandpaper, as necessary for proper fit.

8 Paint or stain box and wood trims, if contrasting trim is desired.

9 Predrill nail holes in hardwood moldings that will be secured with brads, using 1/16" (1.5 mm) drill bit. Apply bead of glue to back of moldings. Position on box; clamp until dry, or secure with brads.

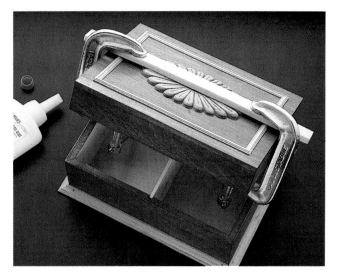

10 Secure decorative wood medallions, if desired, using wood glue; clamp until dry. To protect wood trims from clamps, use a scrap of lumber as shown.

11 Countersink brads, using nail set. Paint or stain the box as desired; if stain is used, fill the nail holes with matching putty.

209

TROMPE L'OEIL BOXES

Decoratively painted wooden boxes can accent desks, countertops, and end tables as well as provide needed storage for small items. Designs painted in trompe l'œil, which means "fool the eye," add whimsy to simple wooden boxes. On the following pages, the instructions and any necessary patterns are given for three designs with a trompe l'œil effect. Choose either a box tied with a ribbon bow, a wrapped parcel, or a stationery box.

Use unfinished wooden boxes with hinges, available at craft stores in a variety of sizes. Or decorate boxes found at garage sales or gift shops. If you choose an unfinished box, sand it as necessary, and use a primer

before applying the base coat of paint. If painting a box with a varnished surface, lightly sand the surfaces to ensure good paint adhesion.

Use good-quality brushes to achieve even edges and fine lines. Test the paints for proper consistency; a detailed design is often easier to achieve with slightly thinned paints.

To protect the painted finish on the box, apply an aerosol acrylic sealer, available in matte and gloss finishes. A matte finish is recommended for the parcel box; either a matte or a gloss finish is appropriate for the bow and stationery boxes.

MATERIALS

- Wooden box.
- Graphite paper.
- Acrylic paints.
- Artist brushes, such as a flat shader and a liner.
- Fine permanent-ink pen.
- Stationery, to use as pattern guide for stationery box.
- Aerosol acrylic sealer.

Trompe l'œil designs (below) are painted on wooden boxes to create a stationery box, a wrapped parcel, and a box tied with a ribbon bow.

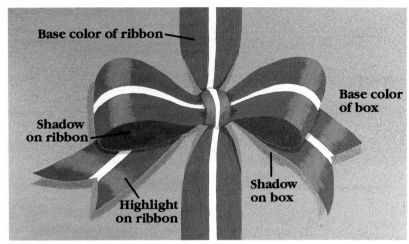

Base color of ribbon

Base color of box

Shadow on ribbon

Shadow on box

Highlight on ribbon

Highlights and shadows add a dimensional effect to painted designs. To paint the highlights, mix white paint with the design's base color. For example, add highlights to a red bow by mixing white paint with red. To paint the shadows, use a darker shade of the base color or mix black with the base color. For example, use a darker red for the shadows inside the loop of the bow; use a darker brown for the shadows that are on top of the box.

VIA AIR MAIL
PAR AVION

1 Apply base coats of paint; allow to dry. Transfer bow design (page 215) to top of box, using graphite paper.

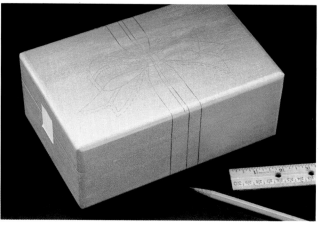

2 Tape box closed at ends. Using pencil, lightly mark ribbon placement by extending lines from bow, 1⅛" (2.8 cm) wide, along top, front, and back of box. For stripes of ribbon, mark lines ½" (1.3 cm) from ribbon placement lines.

3 Paint outer stripes of ribbon using artist's brush, such as a flat shader. Allow paint to dry.

4 Paint the center stripe of the ribbon; allow to dry.

5 Mix a lighter shade of the colors used for the ribbon, using white paint. Highlight the ribbon as shown, to add dimension.

6 Paint a shadow effect on the ribbon as shown, using a darker shade of the ribbon color and thinning the paint for a translucent effect. Paint shadow effect on box as shown, using a darker shade of box color and thinning the paint. Apply aerosol acrylic sealer, if desired.

HOW TO PAINT A PARCEL BOX

1 Apply base coats of paint; allow to dry. Tape box closed. Using pencil, lightly mark fold lines of paper as shown, on opposite sides of box.

2 Mark placement for string along sides and top of box, drawing knot at center of box top.

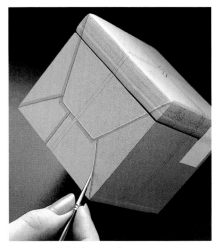

3 Paint fold lines of paper, using darker shade of box color; do not paint where string will overlap fold lines. Allow to dry. Paint highlights and shadows as shown.

4 Apply white paint along marked lines for string; allow to dry. Paint highlights and shadows on one side of string; paint the center knot detail.

5 Mark area for the postage stamp; transfer stamp design (page 215), using graphite paper.

6 Paint stamp, using thinned paint. When dry, paint the lettering and price on stamp, using a permanent-ink pen.

7 Transfer and paint additional labels (page 215) on box, taking care not to paint over the string. Apply aerosol acrylic sealer, if desired.

HOW TO PAINT A STATIONERY BOX

1 Paint or stain box; allow to dry. Mark lines for belt, 1" the (2.5 cm) apart and centered on box, around the top, front, and back. Paint belt, using brown paint; allow paint to dry. Transfer belt details, key, and eyeglasses (opposite) onto box, using graphite paper. Mark placement of eyeglass chain. Mark ¼" (6 mm) strips around the box at lower edge of the top and 1" (2.5 cm) from lower edge of box.

2 Paint the strips around the box, using black paint. Paint the buckle, key, and eyeglasses, using gold paint; for eyeglass chain, use wooden end of brush to paint dots. Paint highlights and shadows of items as shown.

3 Complete belt details, and paint ribbon for key. Paint highlights and shadows as shown.

4 Tape stationery to the top of the box; trace to mark placement. Mark ¼" (6 mm) border on top of box, 1" (2.5 cm) from edges.

5 Paint and outline the stationery. Paint postage stamp as on page 213, steps 5 and 6. Write address on envelope, using permanent-ink marking pen.

6 Transfer fountain pen and stationery design (opposite). Paint border on top of box, fountain pen, and stationery design, using black and gold paints. Paint shadows and highlights. Apply aerosol acrylic sealer, if desired.

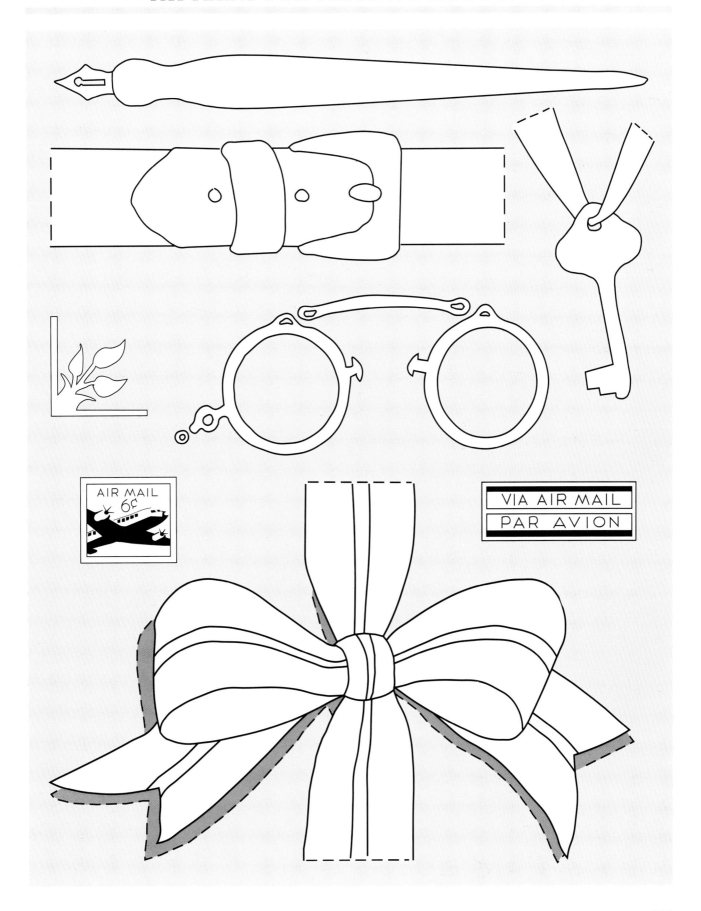

AIR MAIL
6¢

VIA AIR MAIL
PAR AVION

COVERED BOXES

Boxes in all shapes and sizes can be covered with fabric to make pretty room accessories and provide useful storage space. Look for sturdy, smooth cardboard boxes with lids that do not fit too tightly. Computer-paper boxes and packing boxes work well. Chipboard or bristol board, purchased from stationery supply stores can also be used for making boxes. If the cardboard has a smooth, glossy surface on one side, this side can be used for the inside of the box, eliminating the need for lining.

For smoother edges on a corrugated cardboard box, wrap white tape around the edges of the box and cover any overlapped layers of cardboard or seams with white tape before applying the fabric. For durability, heavier cardboards should be used for larger boxes. Or boxes can be reinforced by gluing additional layers of cardboard to the sides before the box is covered.

Fabric may be applied to large surfaces with a spray adhesive, which covers the surfaces quickly without buildup. However, spray adhesive dries quickly, allowing little time for manipulating fabric. For this reason, fabric glue thinned with water works better for smaller areas. Apply the diluted glue to the fabric, using a flat paintbrush. When using spray adhesive, protect the surface from overspray by placing newsprint under the project.

Cover *an under-the-bed storage box to coordinate with your bedroom decor.*

MAKING A BOX

MATERIALS FOR COVERED BOXES

- Chipboard, 10-ply poster board, or bristol board, for small boxes; 14-ply or 16-ply board, for larger boxes; or purchased cardboard or wooden bandboxes.

- Artist's knife.

- White tape, 1" (2.5 cm) wide.

- Mediumweight, firmly woven fabrics for outer fabric and lining; polyester fleece.

- Spray adhesive, intended for fabric use.

- Fabric glue, such as Sobo®, diluted slightly with water for easier spreading.

- Flat paintbrush or disposable foam brush for applying glue.

- Ribbon for covering raw edges of fabric on inside of boxes, optional.

- ½" (1.3 cm) fusible web, for bandboxes.

CUTTING DIRECTIONS

Determine desired finished width and length of box; add twice the desired box depth to these measurements. Draw rectangle to this size on cardboard; cut, using artist's knife or rotary cutter. Repeat for the box lid, making the lid ¼" (6 mm) wider and longer than box measurements; depth of lid may vary, as desired. When cutting with an artist's knife, it is better to use a few medium-pressure cuts rather than one heavy cut.

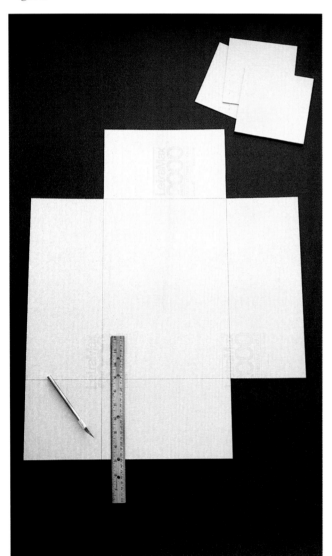

1 Mark the sides of the box on outside of cardboard, using a pencil. Score along the marked lines, using straightedge and artist's knife to cut cardboard lightly; do not cut through. Cut out corner areas of cardboard, using an artist's knife.

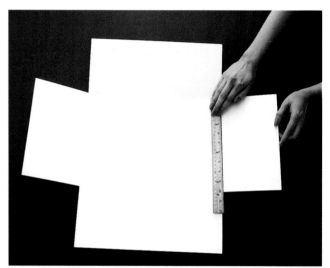

2 Fold sides, supporting cardboard on straightedge or edge of table along scored line, to keep folds straight.

3 Tape sides together, using white tape. Construct lid, using the same method as for the box, except make lid ¼" (6 mm) wider and longer than box measurements.

LINING THE BOX

CUTTING DIRECTIONS

Cut the side lining piece wide enough to wrap around the four sides of the box plus 1" (2.5 cm) for overlap. The length of the side lining piece is equal to the desired depth plus ½" (1.3 cm) to allow the lining to extend onto the bottom of the box. Piece the side lining, if necessary, by overlapping and gluing pieces together.

Cut a piece of cardboard for the bottom of the box ¼" (6 mm) smaller than the length and width of the inside measurement of the box; round the corners. Cut the bottom lining piece 2" (5 cm) larger than the cardboard. Cut a piece of polyester fleece slightly larger than the cardboard bottom.

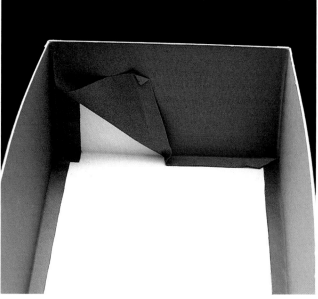

1 Apply spray adhesive to wrong side of side lining piece; affix lining to inside of box, overlapping ½" (1.3 cm) of lining onto bottom of box. Push fabric into corners and lower edge of box; miter bottom corners.

2 Apply spray adhesive to one side of fleece; affix fleece to one side of cardboard bottom. Trim edges even with cardboard.

3 Center cardboard, fleece side down, on wrong side of bottom lining piece. Trim corners of fabric diagonally. Wrap fabric around cardboard at corners and sides; glue in place.

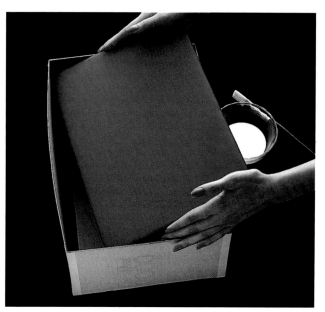

4 Glue covered cardboard inside bottom of box.

COVERING THE BOX

CUTTING DIRECTIONS

For the outside of the box, cut two side pieces, with each piece equal to the width of the side plus 2" (5 cm); cut two end pieces, each equal to the width of the box end minus ¼" (6 mm). The length of the side and end pieces is equal to the depth of the box plus 1" (2.5 cm) to allow fabric to wrap around bottom of box plus the desired amount for wrapping around to the inside of the box. Cut fabric piece for bottom of box ¼" (6 mm) smaller than the width and length of the outside measurement of the box bottom. Cut a length of ribbon equal to distance around box plus 1" (2.5 cm).

1 Apply spray adhesive to wrong side of one side piece; affix to side of box, wrapping 1" (2.5 cm) of fabric around ends and bottom of box. Wrap the remaining fabric to inside of box; affix.

2 Turn box over. Miter corners on bottom of box; affix, using diluted fabric glue. Repeat for the remaining side piece.

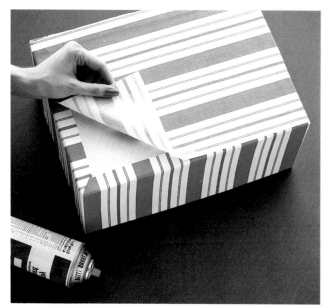

3 Apply spray adhesive to wrong side of end piece; affix to ends of box, wrapping 1" (2.5 cm) of fabric around bottom of box and wrapping remaining fabric to inside of box at upper edge. Apply spray adhesive to wrong side of bottom fabric; affix to bottom of box.

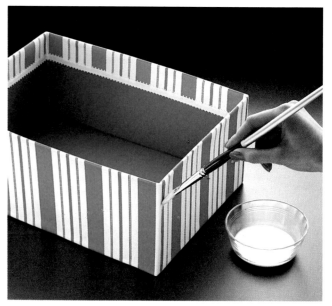

4 Apply diluted fabric glue to one side of ribbon. Affix over raw edge of fabric on inside of box. Seal raw edges of fabric by applying diluted fabric glue.

COVERING THE LID

CUTTING DIRECTIONS

Cut a piece of fabric for the box lid, with the length of the fabric equal to the length of the lid plus four times the lid depth plus 1" (2.5 cm). The width of the fabric is equal to the width of the lid plus four times the lid depth plus 1" (2.5 cm). Cut a piece of fabric ¼" (6 mm) smaller than the underside of the lid.

1 Apply spray adhesive to wrong side of fabric for lid. Center the lid top over fabric; affix. On ends, cut fabric ⅛" (3 mm) in from corner. On sides, cut fabric 1" (2.5 cm) beyond corner, angling to first cut.

2 Affix fabric to long sides of lid, wrapping it around the edge to the inside. Affix corners to ends of lid, using diluted fabric glue.

3 Affix fabric to ends of lid, wrapping it around edge to inside.

4 Apply spray adhesive to wrong side of fabric for underside of lid; affix. Seal raw edges by applying diluted fabric glue.

COVERING BANDBOXES

CUTTING DIRECTIONS

Trace the top of the lid on the wrong side of the outer fabric, polyester fleece, and lining. Cut outer fabric and fleece ½" (1.3 cm) outside the marked line; cut lining ⅛" (3 mm) inside the marked line. Trace the bottom of the box on the wrong side of the outer fabric; cut ⅛" (3 mm) inside the marked line.

Cut a strip of fabric for the lid, with the length of the strip equal to the circumference of the lid lip plus 1"

(2.5 cm); the width of the strip is equal to three times the depth of the lid lip plus ½" (1.3 cm). Cut ½" (1.3 cm) strip of fusible web the length of fabric strip.

Cut a piece of fabric for the box side, with the length of the piece equal to the circumference of the box plus 1" (2.5 cm). The width of the piece is equal to the height of the box plus 1½" (3.8 cm). Cut ½" (1.3 cm) strip of fusible web the width of fabric piece.

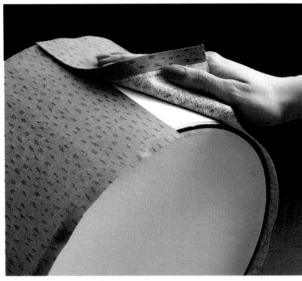

1 Turn under ½" (1.3 cm) along one short end of box side piece; fuse in place, using fusible web. Place side of box on wrong side of fabric, with ½" (1.3 cm) extending beyond bottom of box. Affix fabric to side of box, starting at short end and lapping folded end over raw edge; use spray adhesive for larger boxes, diluted glue for smaller boxes.

2 Clip lower edge of fabric at ½" to 1" (1.3 to 2.5 cm) intervals, to within ⅛" (3 mm) of bottom edge. Glue clipped edges to bottom of box. Apply spray adhesive to wrong side of fabric circle for bottom of box. Center fabric circle over box; affix.

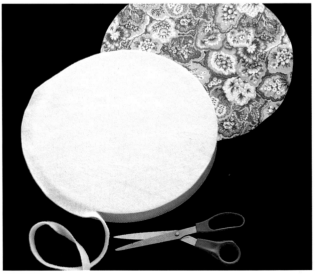

3 Turn box right side up. Glue remaining fabric to inside of box. Glue ribbon over raw edge.

4 Apply spray adhesive to one side of fleece; affix to top of lid. Trim fleece even with edge of lid.

5 Spray other side of fleece. Center lid over outer-fabric circle for lid; affix. Clip fabric at ½" to 1" (1.3 to 2.5 cm) intervals, to within ⅛" (3 mm) of lid edge. Glue clipped edges to lid lip, using diluted fabric glue, lightly pulling fabric taut.

6 Press under one long edge of fabric strip for lid, wrong sides together, an amount equal to the depth of the lid lip. Insert strip of fusible web between fabric layers up to foldline; fuse in place.

7 Glue fabric strip to lid lip, placing fold at upper edge and overlapping ends of strip. Seal raw edge of fabric by applying diluted fabric glue.

8 Clip lower edge of fabric strip up to ⅜" (1 cm) from raw edge; clips should be spaced ½" to 1" (1.3 to 2.5 cm) apart. Wrap fabric around edge to inside; glue in place with clipped edges on underside of lid.

9 Apply spray adhesive to lining circle; affix inside lid, smoothing in place.

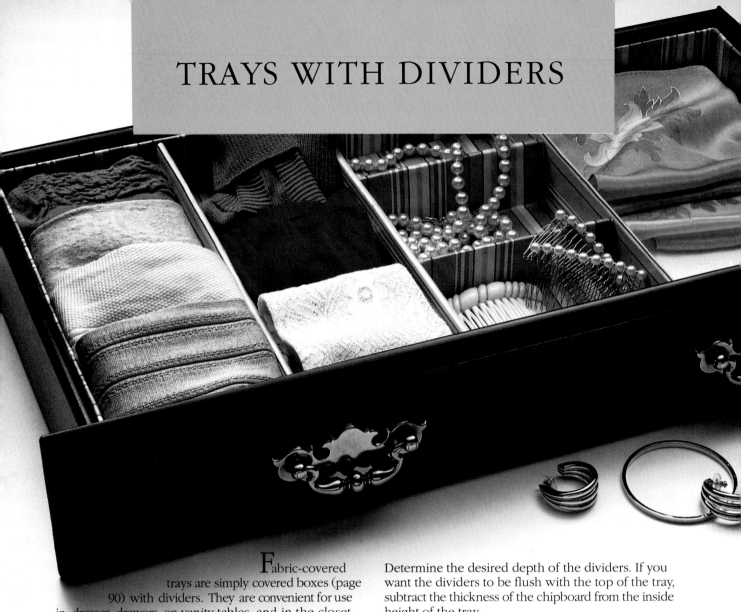

TRAYS WITH DIVIDERS

F abric-covered trays are simply covered boxes (page 90) with dividers. They are convenient for use in dresser drawers, on vanity tables, and in the closet. Boxes divided into larger sections can be used to separate socks and lingerie items; those with smaller sections can be used for items such as jewelry. When used as liners in wire-grid closet storage units, they prevent small items from falling through the grid.

Determine the desired depth of the dividers. If you want the dividers to be flush with the top of the tray, subtract the thickness of the chipboard from the inside height of the tray.

Determine the placement for the sections. When making boxes with dividers, measure and complete each section before measuring for the next divider to ensure the correct amount of ease.

MAKING TRAYS WITH DIVIDERS

MATERIALS

• Materials as listed on page 218. Chipboard is recommended for this project.

CUTTING DIRECTIONS

Cut chipboard for tray following box instructions (page 218). For the outside of the tray, cut two side pieces from fabric, with each piece equal to the width of the side plus 2" (5 cm). Cut two end pieces, each equal to the width of the tray end minus ¼" (6 mm). The length of the side and end pieces is equal to twice the depth of the tray plus 2" (5 cm) to allow fabric to wrap around

bottom of tray on the outside and onto the floor of the tray on the inside. Cut a fabric piece for the bottom of the tray ¼" (6 mm) smaller than the width and length of the outside measurement.

Determine the placement of the sections. Sketch a diagram, including tray measurements, as shown in step 3. Cut chipboard for each divider, with the length of the chipboard equal to the length of the section plus twice the depth of each divider. The width of the chipboard is equal to the width of the section.

Cut a fabric piece for each divider 1" (2.5 cm) wider and longer than the chipboard.

1 Make tray (page 218). Apply spray adhesive to wrong side of one side piece of fabric; affix to side of tray, wrapping 1" (2.5 cm) of fabric around ends and bottom of tray. Miter corners on bottom of tray; affix, using diluted fabric glue. Repeat for remaining side piece.

2 Wrap remaining fabric to inside of tray, mitering corners on floor of tray; affix, using diluted fabric glue. Apply end and bottom pieces as in step 3 on page 220. Seal raw edges of fabric by applying diluted fabric glue.

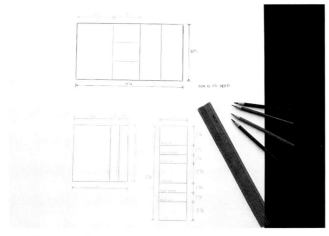

3 Sketch a diagram showing size of sections and placement of dividers; mark tray measurements on sketch. Cut chipboard for first divider, opposite. Mark foldlines on both sides of divider; label which direction divider will be folded on each line.

4 Score along marked lines, using artist's knife and straightedge to cut chipboard lightly. If divider will be folded up, score bottom of divider; if divider will be folded down, score top of divider.

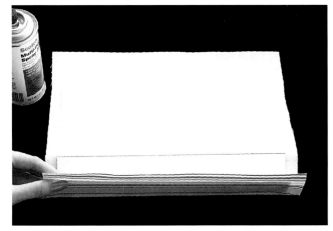

5 Fold divider into shape. Apply spray adhesive or diluted fabric glue to wrong side of fabric; affix fabric to top of shaped divider. Wrap fabric around edges to underside of divider; glue fabric in place.

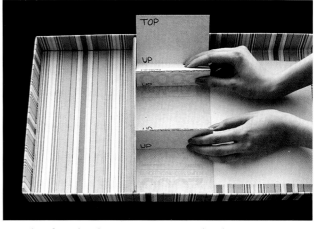

6 Glue first divider in tray. For next divider, measure section and repeat steps, checking fit of divider before covering it with fabric.

DECORATIVE TRAYS

Turn plain trays into stunning accessories by applying a decorative finish. Choose from simplified gilding or a tortoiseshell finish.

Oil-based paints, such as Japan paints, are used for both techniques. Japan paints, available in small containers, are sold at art supply stores and with stenciling supplies at many paint stores.

Gilded designs are applied using precut Mylar® stencils and metallic powder. Apply the metallic powder over a surface of tacky varnish. The result is a stenciled surface that is much smoother and more subtle than that achieved by stenciling with metallic paints. Metallic powders are available at art supply stores in a wide range of colors, from silvery white to rich bronze gold.

A tortoiseshell finish is achieved by streaking thinned varnish stains over a painted base. An orange-red paint, often called barn red, is used for the base coat, and varnish stains in dark oak and black are used for the streaking. The dark oak varnish stain is available at paint and hardware stores, and the black is created by adding black artist's oil color.

Select a tray with smooth, flat surfaces, lightly sanding any prevarnished surfaces to ensure paint adhesion. It is easiest to apply a tortoiseshell finish to a flat, horizontal surface. For this reason, paint the sides of the tray in a solid color and apply the tortoiseshell finish to the bottom only; tape off the sides before working on the bottom of the tray.

Purchased trays *can have a painted tortoiseshell finish, as shown above. Or they can be decorated with a stenciled gilded design and then varnished, as shown opposite.*

HOW TO GILD A TRAY

MATERIALS

- Oil-based paint, such as Japan paint, for base coat.
- Oil-based clear varnish, in gloss or semigloss finish.
- Metallic powder in desired color.
- Precut Mylar® stencil.
- Masking tape.
- Scrap of velvet or chamois leather.

1 Apply a base coat of oil-based paint to a clean, prepared surface; allow to dry. Apply a coat of varnish. Allow varnish to dry about 3 to 5 hours, until slightly tacky; at this time, if the corner of stencil is pressed against the varnish, stencil can be removed with a slight pull, but will leave no mark.

2 Pour a small amount of metallic powder into a bowl. Position stencil in desired location; cover surrounding area on tray by taping paper to stencil.

3 Wrap a scrap of velvet or chamois leather around index finger, wrapping it smoothly so there are no wrinkles or creases at fingertip. Dip wrapped finger into metallic powder; rub on a piece of paper to remove excess powder.

4 Gently rub area to be gilded, starting at the center and working out. As necessary, pick up more powder and reposition stencil. Remove stencil, and allow varnish to dry at least 24 hours.

5 Remove any powder outside design area by rubbing gently with mild abrasive cleanser. Wash the surface gently, using soapy water. Rinse and dry.

6 Seal the gilding by applying a coat of varnish; allow varnish to dry.

HOW TO APPLY A TORTOISESHELL FINISH TO A TRAY

MATERIALS

- Oil-based paints, such as Japan paints, in orange-red and black.
- Dark oak varnish stain, in gloss finish.
- Black artist's oil color in small tube.
- Mineral spirits.
- Two flat 2" (5 cm) paintbrushes; round artist's brush.
- Oil-based clear varnish, in gloss or semigloss finish, optional.
- Masking tape.

1 Apply black paint to sides of tray; allow to dry. Tape off inside lower edge of tray sides, using masking tape.

2 Apply base coat of orange-red paint to bottom of tray; allow to dry. Squeeze a small amount of black oil color into a bowl; dilute with dark oak varnish stain until mixture will flow, and set aside to be used in step 5.

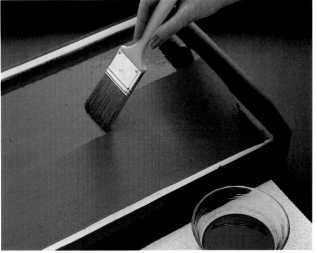

3 Dilute dark oak varnish stain, about one part mineral spirits to two parts varnish; apply over base coat of paint, using flat paintbrush.

(Continued)

4 Brush irregular, diagonal zigzag strokes across the surface of the wet varnish.

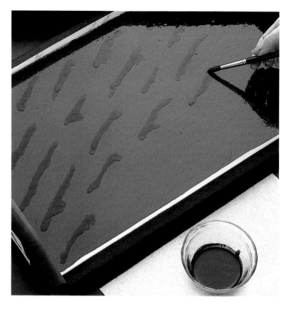

5 Apply diluted black oil color from step 2 in irregular streaks, parallel to diagonal brush strokes and about 2" (5 cm) apart; use a pointed artist's brush and a sideways rolling motion. Allow the surface to harden for 1 to 2 minutes.

6 Stroke the bristle tips of a clean, dry paintbrush gently over the black streaks, in the same direction as they were painted; this will give wispy edges.

7 Repeat step 6, stroking in opposite diagonal direction; this merges some of the streaks. Repeat as necessary to even up the design, taking care not to darken all of the base color.

8 Allow surface to dry. For a more durable finish, apply a coat of clear varnish to bottom and sides of the tray.

MORE IDEAS FOR DECORATIVE TRAYS

Blonde tortoiseshell finish is achieved by applying a base coat of metallic gold paint, followed by a dark oak varnish. Artist's oil colors in burnt umber and black are used for the streaked effect.

Gilded tray with two colors of metallic powder is achieved by using a stencil kit that contains a separate stencil plate for each metallic color.

SLATTED TRAYS

Black lacquered tray is a sophisticated accent on a contemporary table. The stained and painted tray, opposite, has a country look.

Simple in style, this tray is attractive as a decorative accessory on a buffet or side table and sturdy enough to use as a serving tray. The tray is built using stock screen molding and parting stop; simply cut the strips to length. The instructions that follow are for a tray that measures about 11¾" × 18" (30 × 46 cm); the dimensions can be easily changed for a custom size.

Screen molding, generally available in pine and oak, is used for the slats of the base and the runners on the bottom. Parting stop, generally available in pine only, is used for the sides and handles.

The tray may be either stained or painted. Or for another look, stain and paint may be used in combination. For example, if oak screen molding and pine parting stop are used in the same tray, you may prefer to stain the oak and paint the pine.

For ease in finishing, apply the paint or stain before assembling the tray. If you are painting the tray, apply a wood primer before applying a good-quality enamel paint. For a more durable finish on either a stained or painted tray, apply a final coat of nonyellowing varnish or polyurethane sealer.

MATERIALS

- 22 ft. (671 cm) of ¼" × ¾" (6 mm × 2 cm) pine or oak screen molding.
- 5 ft. (152.5 cm) of ½" × ¾" (1.3 × 2 cm) pine parting stop.
- Twelve 6 × 1" (2.5 cm) brass wood screws, for securing runners and handles.
- ¾" (2 cm) brads, for securing the slats.
- 180-grit or 220-grit sandpaper.

- Drill; ¹⁄₁₆" and ³⁄₃₂" drill bits; ⁹⁄₆₄" countersink bit.
- Coping saw; or miter box and backsaw.
- Phillips screwdriver.
- Wood glue.
- Wood stain, or wood primer and enamel paint.
- Nonyellowing varnish or polyurethane sealer, optional.

HOW TO MAKE A SLATTED TRAY

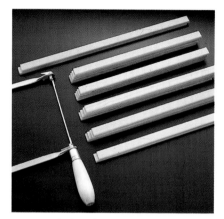

1 Cut 16 slats from screen molding in 11¾" (30 cm) lengths; you may want to cut two or three extra slats in case some split during assembly. Cut two bottom runners from the screen molding in 15¾" (40 cm) lengths.

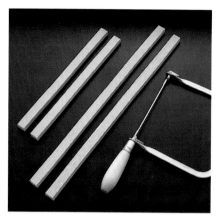

2 Cut two tray handles from parting stop in 11¾" (30 cm) lengths. Cut two tray sides from parting stop in 18" (46 cm) lengths. Round edges at cut ends of all strips by sanding them. Sand sides of strips as necessary. Apply stain, or apply primer and paint.

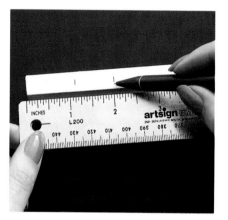

3 Place one side piece with the narrow side up. Using a pencil, lightly mark lines 1⅛" (2.8 cm) and 2" (5 cm) from ends; if markings are in center of strip, they will be less noticeable in finished tray. Repeat for remaining side piece.

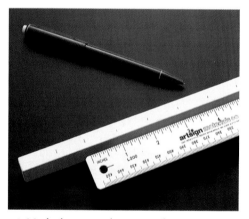

4 Mark the space between the two inner lines at 1" (2.5 cm) intervals. Repeat for remaining side piece.

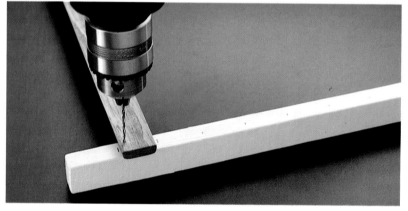

5 Position one tray slat, rounded side down, on side piece, with outer edge of slat aligned with end marking and end of slat extending ⅛" (3 mm) beyond edge of side. Predrill 1/16" (1.5 mm) hole for brad, offsetting hole to allow for later application of screw. Glue slat to side; secure with nail. Repeat for slat at opposite end of side piece.

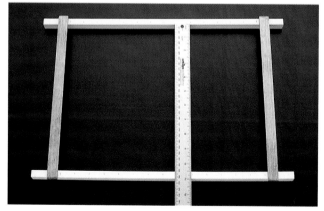

6 Secure remaining side piece to opposite ends of slats, as in step 5, making sure sides are parallel; distance between inside edges of sides is 10½" (27.8 cm).

7 Lay out 14 slats, ¼" (6 mm) apart, between end slats, using marked lines as guides; sides of slats should be ⅛" (3 mm) from marked lines.

8 Predrill and secure slats, securing one slat at a time; start at ends of tray, alternating from side to side, and work toward center. Brads need to be offset on sixth and eleventh slats.

9 Position bottom runners over slats, rounded side up, ⅛" (3 mm) from ends of slats. Predrill holes for screws into end slats, using 3/32" drill bit; drill countersink holes.

10 Predrill holes for screws into sixth and eleventh slats, as in step 9. Glue the runners to the slats; secure the screws, taking care not to overtighten them.

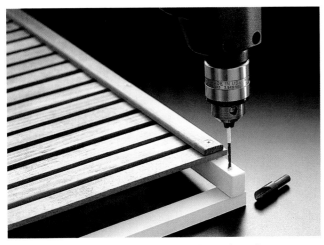

11 Position handles, centered under sides of tray as shown, about ⅛" (3 mm) from ends of side pieces. Predrill holes, 1" (2.5 cm) through the side pieces and handles, using 3/32" drill bit. Drill countersink holes, drilling no farther than necessary to sink screw heads.

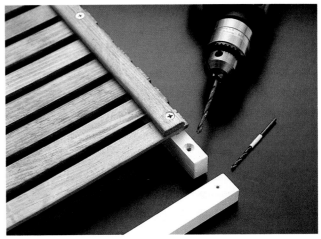

12 Remove handles. Using 9/64" drill bit, drill clearance hole through sides only.

13 Reposition the handles, and secure with wood glue. Insert screws.

14 Apply nonyellowing varnish or polyurethane sealer, if desired.

LEATHER BASKETS & ACCESSORIES

Make a variety of leather accessories, including no-sew laced pillows, custom-sized picture frames, and sturdy baskets. If vegetable-tanned leather is used, the accessories may be stained or personalized with stamped designs.

For laced pillows, select soft, supple leather or suede; a synthetic leather or suede may also be used. For baskets, use a stiff leather, about ⅛" (3 mm) thick, that will provide sufficient support for the sides and handle. For the laced picture frames, made by lacing three layers of leather together, use a stiff leather for the frame back and stand, to provide the proper support; a softer, lightweight leather or suede may be used for the frame front.

The leather skins and any necessary supplies are available at leather craft and supply stores. For the laced edges of pillows and picture frames and the ties on leather baskets, leather and suede lacing is available in various widths. To determine the amount of lacing needed for a laced pillow, allow about three times the distance to be laced, plus 1¼ yd. (1.15 m) for knotted ends. For a picture frame, allow about four times the distance around the outside of the frame. For the ties on a leather basket, 2 yd. (1.85 m) of lacing is used.

A punch tool and mallet are used to make lacing holes in leather quickly and easily. Punch tools are available in many sizes; a size 4, or ⁵⁄₃₂" (3.8 mm), punch tool will work for most lacing. Saddle-stamping tools, available in a variety of designs, are used for making stamped designs on heavyweight vegetable-tanned leather. When punching and stamping leather, work on a hard, smooth surface, such as a sturdy workbench or a piece of firm Masonite® or marble.

For aligning stamped designs, a placement line may be lightly scored on the leather with your fingernail. Do not draw the line with a pencil, because pencil markings often cannot be removed without marring the leather. A pencil may be used for marking lacing holes that will be punched out of the leather.

Special leather stains are available in several shades. They not only change the color of a vegetable-tanned leather, they also bring out the grain and enhance any stamped designs. Before applying stain to a project, test it on a scrap of the leather you will be using. If stain is being applied to a lightweight leather, some shrinkage may occur. Leather finishes are also available; they provide a durable, water-repellent finish and a soft luster.

MATERIALS

- Leather.
- Leather lacing.
- Leather round-drive punch tool, in size appropriate for lacing; a size 4, or ⁵⁄₃₂", will work for most leather lacing.
- Two-pronged leather-lacing needle.
- Mallet, of wood, rubber, or rawhide.
- Mat knife or rotary cutter; metal straightedge.
- Pillow form, in desired size, for pillow.
- Decorative beads, optional, for pillow.
- Cardboard, optional, for frame.
- Saddle-stamping tools, for stamped designs.
- Leather stain, optional.
- Leather finish.

Leather accessories, *such as a laced pillow and frame and a stamped basket, give a room the rustic look of a country lodge.*

HOW TO MAKE A LEATHER BASKET

1 Cut 12" (30.5 cm) square of paper; fold to divide into fourths, then eighths. Using a compass at folded center point, draw a circle with 5¾" (14.5 cm) radius; cut. Mark placement for lacing holes on folds, ¼" (6 mm) from outer edge.

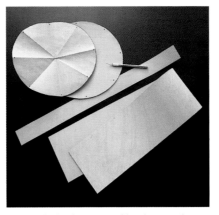

2 Mark the bottom of basket, and cut from leather with rotary cutter or mat knife, using paper pattern as a guide; transfer markings for holes. Cut 6" × 37" (15 × 94 cm) leather strip for sides. Cut 2" × 24" (5 × 61 cm) leather strip for handle.

3 Mark eight holes, ¼" (6 mm) from lower edge of side piece and 4⅜" (11.2 cm) apart, with the first hole 3" (7.5 cm) from end. Punch holes in the bottom and side piece of the basket at markings.

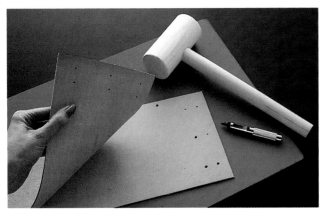

4 Mark three holes, ⅝" (1.5 cm) from short end of side piece, 1" (2.5 cm) from the top, at center, and 1" (2.5 cm) from the bottom. Mark a second row of three holes, ¾" (2 cm) from the first row. Repeat at opposite short end of side piece. Punch holes.

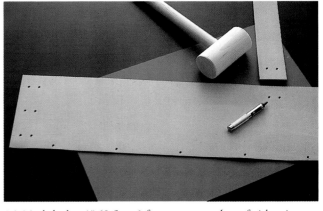

5 Mark holes 1" (2.5 cm) from upper edge of side piece, 18⅛" and 18⅞" (46.3 and 48.2 cm) from one short end; these are used for attaching handle. Mark two holes in handle, 1" (2.5 cm) from short end and ⅝" (1.5 cm) from long edges; repeat at opposite end. Punch holes.

6 Stamp, stain, and finish the leather, if desired (page 241). Overlap short ends of side strip, aligning the holes. Secure side piece at each pair of holes, using 6" (15 cm) lengths of lacing; attach the handle to inside of the basket when securing the upper edge. Attach the handle at other side of the basket, using 6" (15 cm) length of lacing.

7 Secure the side piece to basket bottom at holes, using 6" (15 cm) lengths of lacing. Trim ends of lacing, if desired.

HOW TO MAKE A LACED LEATHER PILLOW

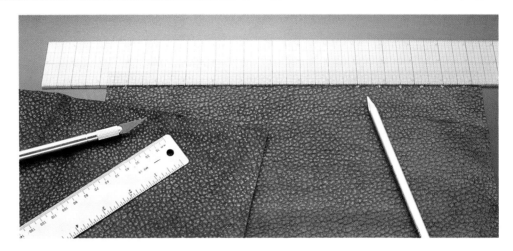

1 Cut the pillow front and pillow back from leather, using a metal straightedge and a mat knife or rotary cutter, cutting pieces 1" (2.5 cm) wider and longer than pillow form. Using chalk or lead pencil, mark placement for lacing holes on top side of pillow front, ⅝" (1.5 cm) from the edges; position a hole at each corner and at intervals of ¾" to 1" (2 to 2.5 cm).

2 Punch holes for lacing in pillow front, using punch tool and mallet. Place the pillow front on pillow back, top sides together. Using pillow front as a guide, mark holes on top side of pillow back. Punch holes.

3 Cut a length of lacing equal to three times the length of first side to be laced plus 12" (30.5 cm). Using mat knife, trim end of lacing to a point.

4 Open the leather needle at the spring end; insert the lacing with top side of lacing against the prongs. Using needlenose pliers, squeeze the needle so prongs pierce lacing.

5 Place pillow front on pillow back, top sides facing out. Using whipstitch, lace the first side; leave about 6" (15 cm) tails at ends. Repeat to lace three sides of pillow.

6 Insert pillow form. Lace the remaining side. Tie ends of lacing at corners. Attach beads, if desired, securing them with overhand knot.

HOW TO MAKE A LACED LEATHER FRAME

1 Determine size of picture opening; picture can be no more than ¼" (6 mm) wider than opening. To length and width, add 2¾" (7 cm) to allow for 1⅜" (3.5 cm) borders; this is finished size. Cut two pieces of stiff leather equal to the finished size, using mat knife; these will be frame back and stand. Cut a third piece for frame front; this may be cut from leather of a lighter weight. Mark picture opening on frame front; cut.

2 Mark placement for lacing holes on top side of frame front, ½" (1.3 cm) from edges, using pencil or chalk; position a hole at each corner and at regular intervals of about ¾" (2 cm). Punch holes, using a punch tool and a mallet. Place the frame front on the frame stand, top sides together. Using the frame front as a guide, mark holes on the frame stand. Punch holes.

3 Mark and punch holes on frame back; at lower edge, punch only one hole in from each corner hole. This leaves opening for inserting picture. Stamp, stain, and finish the leather, if desired (opposite).

4 Position frame front on back, top sides facing out. Secure lacing to leather needle as on page 238, step 4. Insert needle from back of frame, into hole about one-third the distance from the top; leave tail for knotting ends.

5 Lace the frame together, using whipstitch, along first side and lower edge; at opening on lower edge, lacing is done through frame front only.

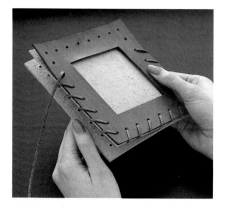

6 Lace the remaining side to hole opposite starting point. Position frame stand against frame back, with top sides facing out.

7 Lace through all layers of frame to attach stand to upper portion of sides and along top edge.

8 Continue lacing around the frame stand only.

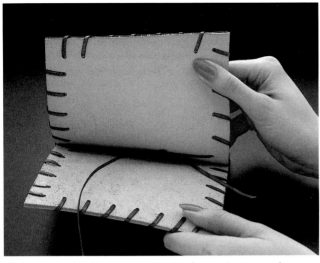

9 Bring ends of lacing across the frame, between frame back and frame stand; tie ends together. Trim tails.

10 Insert the picture into laced frame.

HOW TO STAMP, STAIN & FINISH LEATHER

1 **Stamp.** Prepare leather by wiping both sides with a dampened sponge; place in plastic bag, and allow to set several hours. Remove leather from bag; allow surface of leather to dry, just until original leather color returns.

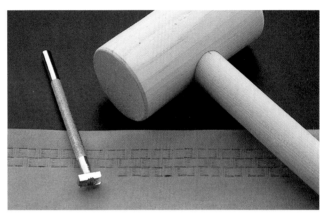

2 Place leather on hard, smooth surface, top side up. Position saddle-stamping tool on leather; pound with mallet until imprint is clear.

Stain. Stamp leather, if desired. Apply a liberal coat of leather stain to leather, using a rag and circular motion; allow to set several minutes. Remove excess stain, using a dampened sponge; if leather is stamped, stain should remain in crevices of stamped design. Allow to dry.

Finish. Apply an even, light coat of leather finish, using dampened sponge; allow to dry. Apply second coat of finish. When dry, buff leather with soft rag.

MORE IDEAS FOR LEATHER ACCESSORIES

Albums and note pads *with leather covers are embellished with twigs and beads, inserted into the lacing.*

Colorful assortment of suedes *is used to make a collection of frames; contrasting black lacing unifies the frames.*

242

Strips of leather *are pieced together on the diagonal for this pillow front. Overlap the strips, and stitch, using a leather needle. Or glue the strips, using a leather cement.*

Animal skin *is used for the front of a laced pillow. Mark and punch the holes from the back side of the skin.*

Pair of baskets *adds texture to a rustic decorating scheme. The smaller basket is stamped in an all-over design. The larger basket has an added strip of textured leather laced near the top.*

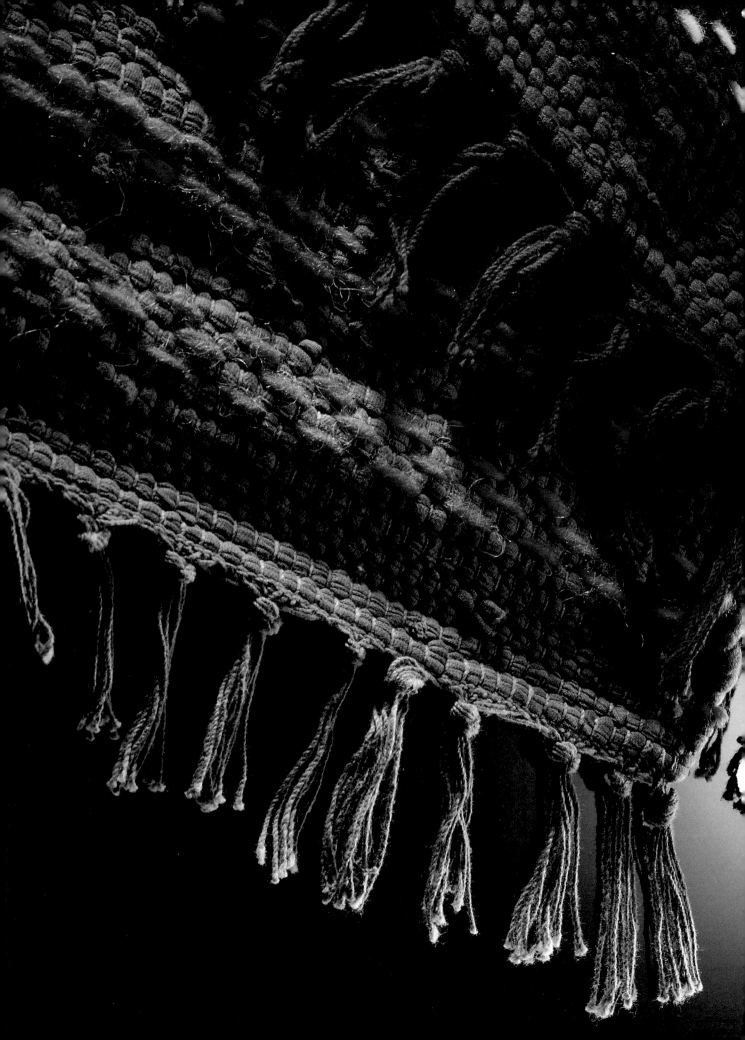

Coverings for Furniture & Floors

RUFFLED STOOL COVERS

Wooden stools make convenient seating at a breakfast nook or counter, either for casual dining or for resting while you prepare food. Padded with foam, this ruffled stool cover adds comfort to a wooden stool.

Ruffled stool covers can be made for stools that are already padded, or the padding can be included in the stool cover. To add padding to the stool cover, use polyurethane foam.

The instructions that follow include a self-lined skirt, which adds body and eliminates the need for a hem. If a heavyweight fabric is used, the skirt may be cut shorter and narrow-hemmed instead.

HOW TO SEW A RUFFLED STOOL COVER

MATERIALS

- Mediumweight fabric; 1½ yd. (1.4 m) is usually sufficient for one stool cover.
- Cording, for welting; 1½ yd. (1.4 m) is usually sufficient for one stool cover.
- Cord, such as pearl cotton, for gathering the ruffle.
- Polyurethane foam, 2" (5 cm) thick.
- Upholstery batting.

CUTTING DIRECTIONS

Make a pattern for cutting the foam by tracing around the top of the wooden stool. Mark a circle this size on the foam; cut the foam, using an electric knife or serrated knife.

For the cover top, cut one circle of fabric, 1" (2.5 cm) larger than the top of the stool, to allow for ½" (1.3 cm) seam allowance.

For the side of the stool cover, cut a boxing strip 1" (2.5 cm) wider than the thickness of the foam, with the length of the boxing strip 1" (2.5 cm) longer than the circumference around the top of the stool.

For a self-lined ruffled skirt with a finished length of 5" (12.5 cm), cut a rectangle of fabric on the crosswise or lengthwise grain, 11" (28 cm) wide by twice the circumference of the stool, piecing the strip, if necessary.

For the welting around the cover top, cut 1½" (3.8 cm) bias strips of fabric, with the combined length of the strips equal to the circumference of the stool top plus 3" (7.5 cm).

For the ties that secure the cover to the legs of the stool, cut eight 2½" × 12" (6.5 × 30.5 cm) fabric strips on the lengthwise or crosswise grain; two ties are used at each leg.

1 Join the bias fabric strips for welting. Fold the strip around the cording, wrong sides together, matching raw edges. Using zipper foot, machine-stitch close to cording.

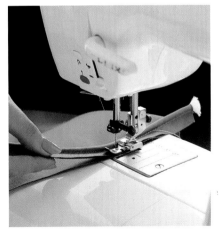

2 Stitch welting to right side of the cover top, over previous stitches on welting, matching raw edges and starting 2" (5 cm) from end of welting; ease welting around curved edge.

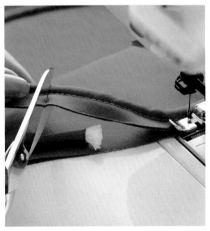

3 Stop stitching 2" (5 cm) from the point where ends of welting will meet. Cut off one end of welting so it overlaps the other end by 1" (2.5 cm).

(Continued)

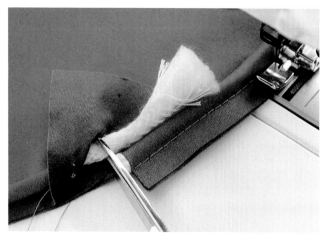

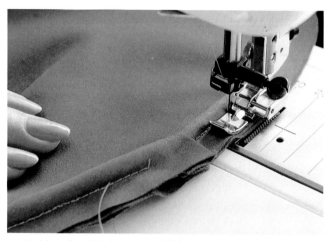

4 Remove the stitching from one end of welting. Trim ends of cording so they just meet.

5 Fold under ½" (1.3 cm) of fabric on overlapping end of welting. Lap it around the other end; finish stitching the welting to the cover top.

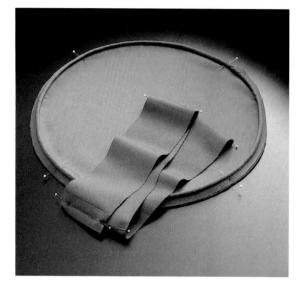

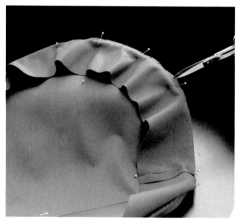

6 Stitch the short sides of boxing strip together, right sides together, in a ½" (1.3 cm) seam; press seam open. Fold the boxing strip into fourths; pin-mark upper and lower edges. Fold cover top into fourths; pin-mark.

7 Pin upper edge of boxing strip to the cover top, matching pin marks; clip boxing strip within seam allowance as necessary, and ease boxing strip to fit.

8 Stitch boxing strip to the cover top in ½" (1.3 cm) seam, taking care to avoid stitching any tucks; stitch with cover top facing up.

9 Stitch the skirt pieces together in ½" (1.3 cm) seams, right sides together; stitch ends together, forming continuous strip. Press seams open.

10 Fold skirt in half lengthwise, wrong sides together; press.

11 Zigzag over a cord, a scant ½" (1.3 cm) from the raw edges of the skirt.

12 Fold skirt into fourths; pin-mark. Align upper edge of skirt to the lower edge of boxing strip, matching pin marks; gather to fit by pulling on the cord. Pin in place, matching raw edges; stitch ½" (1.3 cm) seam.

13 Fold ½" (1.3 cm) to wrong side at one end of tie. Press the tie in half lengthwise, wrong sides together. Fold each edge to the center; press. Refold at center; press. Repeat for remaining ties.

14 Stitch along folded lengthwise edge of tie and across folded end.

15 Divide ruffle seam into fourths; pin-mark. Pin two ties to ruffle at each pin mark; align unfinished ends of ties to raw edge of ruffle. Stitch the ties in place along seamline. Finish seam at lower end of boxing strip, using zigzag or overlock stitch. Omit step 16 if purchased stool has padded seat.

16 Cover the foam with a layer of upholstery batting; hand-baste batting in place. Place foam into cover.

17 Place the cover on the stool with ties at legs of stool. Secure the ties around legs.

BUTTON-TUFTED CUSHIONS

Add seating comfort to wooden chairs and benches with simple knife-edge, button-tufted cushions. The lightly padded inner cushion is created by covering a piece of foam with a layer of polyester upholstery batting. The button tufting prevents the cushion from shifting inside the cover and also adds detailing. Place one button on the top and one on the bottom of the cushion, and pull them tight with strands of thread to create an indentation. Welting can be inserted into the seam for additional interest.

You may want to make the covered buttons and welting from a fabric that contrasts with that of the seat cushion. Checked and striped fabrics can create interesting effects when used for welting.

Secure the seat cushion to the chairs or benches with ties, if necessary. Place a set of ties near each back corner of the cushion for securing it to the back posts of the chair or bench.

HOW TO MAKE A BUTTON-TUFTED CUSHION

MATERIALS

- Decorator fabric.
- Contrasting decorator fabric, for buttons and welting, optional.
- Polyurethane foam, 1" (2.5 cm) thick.
- Polyester upholstery batting; polyester fiberfill, optional.
- Cording, 5/32" (3.8 mm) in diameter, for welting, optional.
- Upholstery buttons or flat dressmaker buttons with strong shank; two for each button placement.
- Buttonhole twist or carpet thread; long needle with large eye.

CUTTING DIRECTIONS

Make the pattern and cut the fabric, foam, and batting following steps 1 to 3, below. For the optional welting, cut 1⅝" (4 cm) bias fabric strips; piece the strips as necessary to make a length that is equal to the circumference of the cushion plus at least 1" (2.5 cm) overlap at the ends. For each tie, cut two 1½" (3.8 cm) fabric strips 10" to 16" (25.5 to 40.5 cm) long.

1 Make a paper pattern of seat to be covered by cushion, rounding any sharp corners; simplify shape as necessary. Cut pattern; check the fit. Mark pattern for placement of ties, if desired.

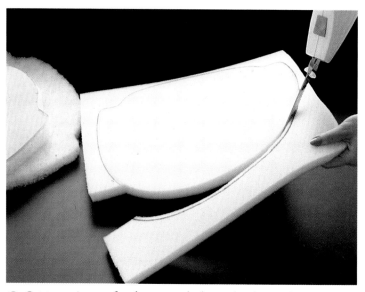

2 Cut two pieces of polyester upholstery batting, using pattern. Position pattern on foam; trace, using marking pen. Cut foam ¼" (6 mm) inside marked line, using electric or serrated knife.

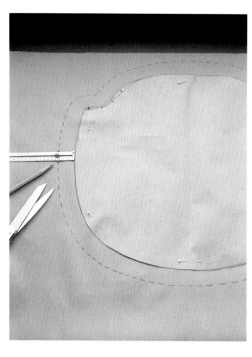

3 Position the pattern on wrong side of decorator fabric. Mark cutting line 1" (2.5 cm) from edge of pattern; this allows ½" (1.3 cm) for the seam allowances and ½" (1.3 cm) for the thickness of the foam and batting. Cut the cushion top on marked line. Cut cushion bottom, using cushion top as pattern.

4 Make welting, if desired, and apply to cushion top. Make ties, if desired, as on page 155, step 3. Pin ties to the right side of seat top at markings, with raw edges even; stitch in place.

5 Position cushion top and bottom with right sides together and raw edges even. Stitch ½" (1.3 cm) seam; leave center opening along back edge for inserting cushion. Trim the seam allowances and clip curves. If welting is not used, press seam open. Turn right side out; lightly press.

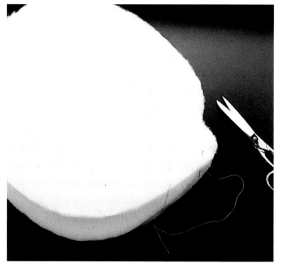

6 Place foam between layers of batting; hand-baste edges of batting together, encasing foam.

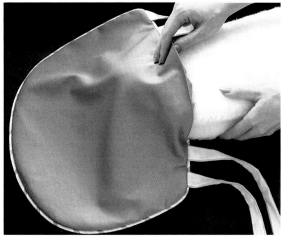

7 Fold the foam in half; insert into fabric cover. Flatten foam, smoothing the fabric over batting. Insert polyester fiberfill into corners, if necessary. Slipstitch opening closed.

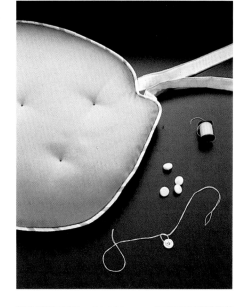

8 Pin-mark button placement on both sides of cushion as desired. Cut two or three 18" (45 cm) strands of buttonhole twist or carpet thread; insert all strands through button shank, and secure at middle of thread length with a double knot.

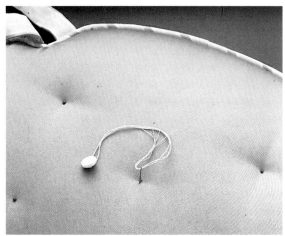

9 Insert the ends of the thread strands through the eye of a long needle. Insert needle through cushion to back side. Remove strands from needle; divide strands into two groups.

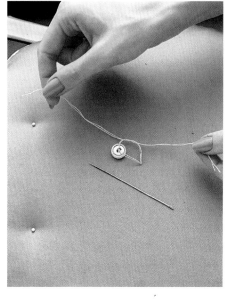

10 Thread second button on one group of threads; tie a single knot, using both thread groups; pull until buttons are tight against cushion, creating indentation. Wrap the thread two or three times around the button shank. Tie a double knot; trim thread tails.

SLIPCOVERS

Two-piece slipcovers can be used on simple kitchen or dining-room chairs to update a look or to help soften the room with fabric. Slipcovers can also be used to cover up worn or unmatched chairs. Slipcover styles can range from country to formal, depending on the fabric choice and detailing of the chair. Both the back and the seat slipcovers are lined for durability and body. Welting, applied around the seat slipcover and along the lower edge of the back slipcover, adds a finishing touch.

The back slipcover and the skirt on the chair seat can be long or short. When determining the desired back length and skirt length of the slipcovers, take into account the style and detailing of the chair. For a nice drape and an attractive appearance, make the skirt at least 5" to 6" (12.5 to 15 cm) long and end the skirt slightly above or below any cross pieces of the chair. Chairs with seats that slope toward the back will have skirts that also slope toward the back, making the fabric hang slightly off-grain at the side back of the chair. For this reason, avoid long skirt styles on chairs that have sloping seats. It may also be desirable to avoid fabrics with obvious stripes, plaids, or one-way designs on chairs of this style.

The seat slipcover can be made with either pleats or clustered gathers at the front corners. Select chairs with an open back at the edge of the seat to allow decorative ties to be secured to the back posts. Concealed twill-tape ties secure the cover to the front legs of the chair.

For back slipcovers that are long, the back of the chair must be straight from the seat to the upper edge of the back or taper slightly inward; if the upper edge of the chair back is wider than the lower edge, it will not be possible to slip the cover on. However, short slipcovers, covering one-third to one-half of the back, may be suitable for this style chair. You may want to test-fit a muslin pattern before purchasing the decorator fabric.

MATERIALS

- Muslin, for patterns.
- Decorator fabric.
- Lining fabric.
- 1" (2.5 cm) twill tape.
- 5⁄32" (3.8 mm) cording, for optional welting.

Slipcovers can be designed to offer either a casual or a formal look. The short, casual slipcovers opposite have skirts with clustered gathers at the front corners. At right, the tailored slipcover has a full-length back and skirt. The skirt features inverted pleats at the front corners.

CUTTING DIRECTIONS

Make the seat and back patterns as on pages 256 and 257. Cut one seat each from outer fabric and lining; transfer the markings. For a gathered skirt, cut the fabric as on page 257, steps 1 and 2. For a skirt with corner pleats, cut the fabric as on page 259, step 1. Cut eight fabric strips 1½" (3.8 cm) wide and 10" to 16" (25.5 to 40.5 cm) long for the back ties on the seat cover. Cut four 12" (30.5 cm) lengths of twill tape for the concealed front ties. Using the pattern for a straight or shaped slipcover back (pages 256 and 257), cut one front and one back from both the outer fabric and lining; transfer the markings.

If welting is desired, cut 1⅝" (4 cm) bias strips. The combined length of the strips is equal to the circumference of the seat cover and the lower edge of the back cover; allow extra for seams and overlaps.

HOW TO MAKE A CHAIR SEAT SLIPCOVER PATTERN

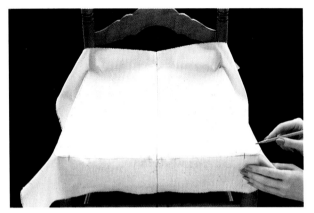

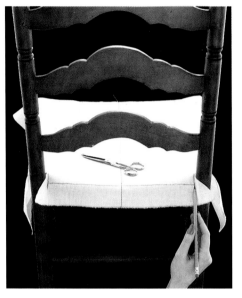

1 Measure the chair seat; cut muslin about 6" (15 cm) larger than measurements. Mark the center line on lengthwise grain. Center muslin on seat; pin or tape in place. Using pencil, mark outer rim of seat front, and sides to back posts, rounding square corners slightly. Mark placement for front ties.

2 Mark back edge of chair seat on muslin; clip the fabric as necessary for snug fit if seat is shaped around back posts. On muslin, mark the placement of skirt back between the chair posts.

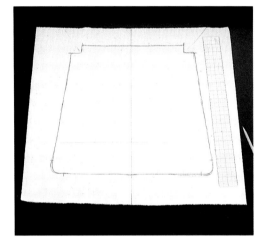

3 Remove muslin from the chair. Redraw seamlines as necessary, using a straightedge; redraw curved lines, drawing smooth curves. Reposition muslin on chair; adjust as necessary.

4 Add ½" (1.3 cm) seam allowances. Cut pattern on marked lines.

HOW TO MAKE A CHAIR BACK SLIPCOVER PATTERN

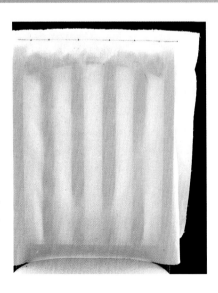

1 Straight upper edge. Measure chair back; cut two pieces of muslin about 6" (15 cm) wider and 2" (5 cm) longer than measurements. Mark a line, 1" (2.5 cm) from raw edge, for upper edge of chair back; pin pieces together on the marked line. Center the muslin on the chair with the marked line at upper edge.

2 Pin muslin at sides of chair, allowing ample ease. Mark desired finished length. Pull gently on cover to make sure it slides off easily; adjust width or length of cover, if necessary.

3 Mark seamlines, following pin placement. Label patterns for front and back.

4 Remove muslin from the chair. Redraw seamlines as necessary, using straightedge. Repin muslin, and position on chair; adjust as necessary. Front and back of pattern may be different sizes.

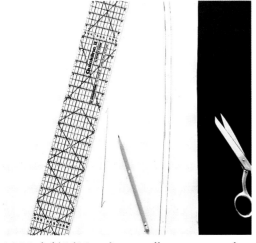

5 Mark ½" (1.3 cm) seam allowances; mark grainline. Cut pattern on marked lines.

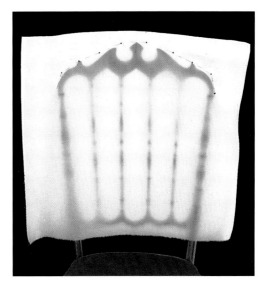

Shaped upper edge. Measure chair back; cut two pieces of muslin about 6" (15 cm) larger than measurements. Pin pieces together at the upper edge, and center over chair back; adjust pins to follow contours of the chair, simplifying design as necessary. Continue as for chair back with straight upper edge, steps 2 to 4, opposite; in step 4, smooth any curved lines. Complete pattern as in step 5.

HOW TO SEW A CHAIR SEAT SLIPCOVER WITH GATHERED CORNERS

1 Measure pattern seamline around the front and sides of seat between markings at the back posts; add 12" (30.5 cm) for the corner gathers plus 1" (2.5 cm) for seam allowances. Cut the fabric strip for front skirt to this length, piecing fabric, if necessary; width of strip is equal to twice the desired finished skirt length plus 1" (2.5 cm) for seam allowances.

2 Measure pattern seamline between markings for back skirt. Cut fabric strip for back skirt to this length plus 1" (2.5 cm); width of strip is equal to twice the desired finished skirt length plus 1" (2.5 cm) for seam allowances.

(Continued)

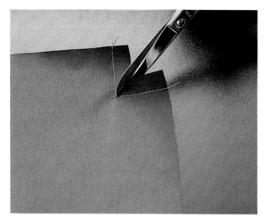

3 Staystitch any inner corners and curves on chair seat top and lining. Clip to, but not through, stitching as necessary.

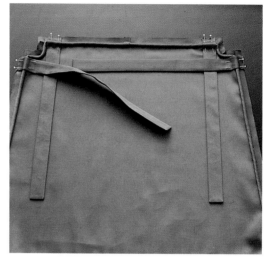

4 Make welting, if desired, and apply to seat top. Stitch strips for decorative ties as on page 155, step 3. Pin ties to the right side of seat top at back corners as desired, aligning raw edges.

5 Fold the skirt front in half lengthwise, right sides together; stitch ½" (1.3 cm) seams on short ends. Turn right side out; press. Repeat for skirt back.

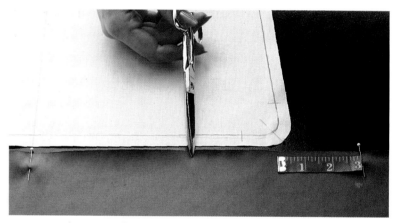

6 Pin-mark center of skirt at raw edges. Measure edge of seat pattern on seamline, from center front to corner; add 3" (7.5 cm). Measure this distance out from center of skirt, and pin-mark for corners. Clip-mark skirt 6" (15 cm) from both sides of corner pin marks.

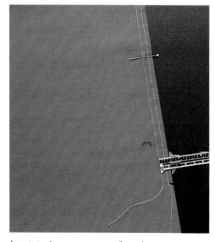

7 Stitch two rows of gathering threads along upper edge of skirt front between clip marks, ¼" (6 mm) and ½" (1.3 cm) from raw edges.

8 Pin skirt front to the seat top, right sides together, matching the raw edges and markings for center front and corners. Pull gathering threads to fit. Machine-baste skirt to seat top, using zipper foot.

9 Pin skirt back to the seat top, right sides together, matching the raw edges; stitch, using zipper foot.

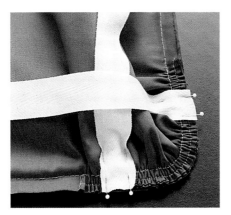

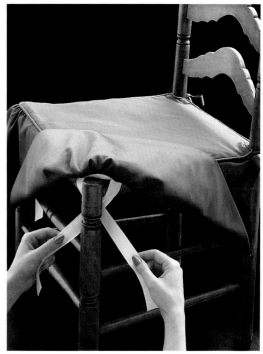

10 Pin or baste twill-tape ties to wrong side of skirt at front-corner tie markings.

11 Pin skirt and ties to the seat to prevent catching them in seam allowance. Pin lining to the seat, with right sides together and raw edges even. Stitch, leaving a 6" (15 cm) center opening on back of seat. Trim seam allowances; clip curves and corners.

12 Turn the seat cover right side out; press. Slipstitch opening closed. Position seat cover on chair; secure the back ties in a bow or a square knot. Lift skirt, and secure front ties; trim excess length.

HOW TO SEW A CHAIR SEAT SLIPCOVER WITH CORNER PLEATS

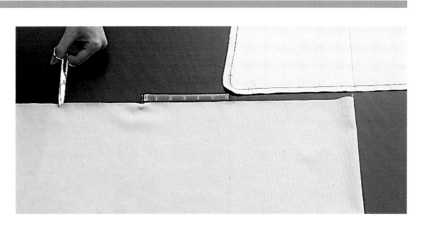

1 Follow steps 1 to 5 on pages 257 and 258; in step 1, add 24" (61 cm) instead of 12" (30.5 cm). Pin-mark the center of the skirt at raw edges. Measure outer edge of seat pattern on seamline, from center front to corner, and add 6" (15 cm); measure this distance from center of skirt front, and pin-mark for corners. Clip-mark the fabric 6" (15 cm) from both sides of the corner pin marks.

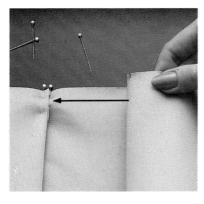

2 Fold 3" (7.5 cm) inverted pleats at front corners, matching the clip marks to the corner pin marks; press. Machine-baste the pleats in place.

3 Pin the skirt front to the seat top, right sides together, matching raw edges and markings for center front and corners; clip skirt at the corners as necessary. Machine-baste skirt to seat top. Complete skirt as in steps 9 to 12, opposite.

HOW TO SEW A CHAIR BACK SLIPCOVER

1 **Straight upper edge.** Place the front and the back outer fabric pieces right sides together, matching the raw edges. Stitch ½" (1.3 cm) seam around sides and upper edge. Press seam open.

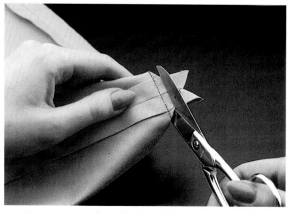

2 To accommodate depth of chair, open out the corners, aligning seam allowances; stitch across corners, a distance equal to the depth of the chair. Trim seam.

3 Attach welting, if desired, to the lower edge of the outer cover. Stitch lining as for outer cover, leaving a 6" (15 cm) center opening on one side. Press seam allowances open.

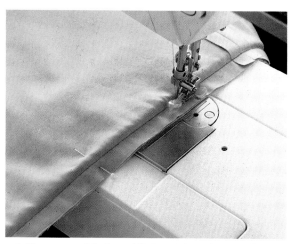

4 Place outer fabric and lining right sides together, matching lower edge; stitch ½" (1.3 cm) seam.

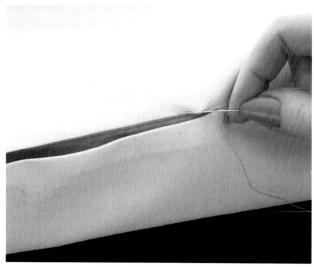

5 Turn slipcover, lining side out, through the opening in the lining; press the lower edge. Slipstitch opening closed. Turn slipcover right side out; place over back of chair.

Shaped upper edge. Place the front and back outer fabric pieces right sides together, matching raw edges. Stitch ½" (1.3 cm) seam around sides and upper edge; press open. Trim seam; clip any curves. Complete as in steps 3 to 5.

MORE IDEAS FOR SLIPCOVERS

Coordinating fabrics are used to cover a pair of unmatched porch chairs (right). One slipcover has a skirt gathered to double fullness. The other slipcover features a skirt with corner pleats. It has additional welting around the sides and upper edge of the chair back. The ties on both chair covers, made 4" (10 cm) wide, create the large bows.

Buttons (below) accent the pleats of the chair skirt and add detail to the lower edge of the back slipcover.

Grosgrain ribbon provides contrast along the lower edges of this chair back and skirt. Apply the grosgrain ribbon by edgestitching along both sides.

YARN-TRIMMED
RUGS

Add colorful detailing to inexpensive, purchased rag rugs with bits of yarn. Concentrate the yarn embellishments at the ends of the rug to create a border, or scatter them throughout the entire rug. As shown opposite, rugs may be trimmed by stitching the yarn into the rug with a simple running stitch (top), weaving it under the rug's warp threads (bottom), or by combining the two techniques (middle).

MATERIALS

- Purchased rag rug.
- Yarn in desired colors.
- Large-eyed yarn needle.

HOW TO EMBELLISH A RUG WITH WOVEN YARNS

1 Thread needle and secure yarn as in step 1, below. Working from side to side across the rug, run needle under warp threads of rug.

2 Leave 1" (2.5 cm) tails of yarn at end of row, if tufted look is desired. Or secure the end of the yarn as in step 3, below.

HOW TO EMBELLISH A RUG WITH RUNNING STITCHES

1 Fold length of yarn in half; thread ends into needle. Working from top of rug, take a small stitch down and up; pull needle through the loop to secure yarn.

2 Sew running stitches, about ½" (1.3 cm) long. If solid row of stitches is desired, repeat running stitches in opposite direction, sewing between previous stitches.

3 Secure stitches at end of row by taking two or three small stitches; conceal end of the yarn by running needle between the rows of the rug.

HOOKED RUGS

Primitive rug hooking is a classic American craft used to make rugs, wall hangings, and pillows. Strips of wool are pulled through a foundation fabric to create a design or picture. The primitive style of hooking, with its simple designs in ¼" (6 mm) wool strips, is easier to master than hooking with narrower strips for more complex designs.

Supplies for rug hooking are minimal and are available at fiber-art stores and through mail-order suppliers. The wool strips may be cut from remnants, discarded garments, or, when necessary, from new pieces of fabric; hand-dyed, color-gradated wool fabrics are also available. To create the muted colors and aged appearance often seen in primitive hooked rugs, the wool fabrics may be simmered in a diluted ammonia solution, a process often referred to as *undyeing* (right).

Cotton monk's cloth is used for the foundation; this fabric is sturdy, flexible, and easy to work with. Cotton twill tape is stitched to the edges of the monk's cloth to prevent raveling during the hooking process; then this same tape is turned under to bind the edges of the completed rug.

In order to achieve even rows of hooked loops, stretch the foundation fabric taut in a frame. A large quilting hoop works well for most small pieces; replace the screw on the outer hoop with a longer screw, if necessary, to allow for additional expansion. Specialized rug-hooking frames, which provide a comfortable working surface, are also available.

Inspiration for designs can come from many sources. Traditional quilt block designs are easily adapted to rug hooking. Patterns from wallpaper, tapestries, and china can also provide design inspiration. Colonial rug designs often featured familiar objects, such as pets, houses, or gardens. Proportion and perspective were not a concern, and the designs often had a whimsical flair.

Start with small, simple designs. A good size for a first project is a wall hanging about 15" (38 cm) square. Select a design that combines various colors and textures. Plaids, herringbones, tweeds, and stripes add texture and create interesting effects. Choose a contrasting background color that allows the design motifs to dominate. In general, the fabric required is about five times the size of the design area.

Prepare the wool fabrics and cotton twill tape by washing them in warm water with a mild detergent, either by hand or by machine in a gentle cycle. Then hang them to dry, or machine dry them. The resulting shrinkage tightens the weave for added strength. Tear or cut the prepared wools into 9" × 12" (23 × 30.5 cm) pieces.

Before starting a project, become familiar with hooking techniques by practicing on a scrap of the foundation fabric, hooking rows in straight lines, curves, and circles. Generally, two threads in the monk's cloth are skipped between the wool loops, and two or three threads are skipped between the rows. If the loops and rows are too close together, the foundation fabric will be stressed and the hooked project will have a lumpy, warped appearance.

Many people prefer to hook the prominent design areas first and any background areas last. You may want to outline a design area by hooking a row of loops around it, then fill in the area with loops. Complete one design area before moving to another.

MATERIALS

- Mediumweight, closely woven fabrics of 100 percent wool.
- Cotton monk's cloth, for foundation.
- Rug hook, in primitive size.
- Rug-hooking frame or wooden quilting hoop.
- Cotton twill tape, 1¼" (3.2 cm) wide, in a color that matches or blends with outer edge of design.
- Heavy-duty cotton thread that matches twill tape.
- Rotary cutter and cutting mat, or sharp scissors.
- Permanent-ink marking pen; transfer pencil; masking tape.
- Mild liquid detergent.

Undyeing is a process that creates muted colors in wool; this gives the wool an aged appearance. Simmer the fabrics for at least 10 minutes in a solution of 1 tsp. (5 mL) ammonia per 1 qt. (0.9 L) water. Rinse the fabric in warm water; then simmer it for 20 minutes in fresh water, with ⅓ c. (79 mL) vinegar added to the water, to set the new color. Rinse the fabric thoroughly; then line dry or machine dry it.

TIPS FOR RUG HOOKING

Mark the colors on the paper pattern, if desired. This is especially helpful for detailed designs.

Strips may be pulled out and rehooked as necessary. Before rehooking, lightly scratch the foundation with your finger to restore the even weave of the fabric.

Vary the direction of the rows within each design area to add a textural effect. This is also used to add interest to large background areas.

Hook at least two rows parallel to and as close as possible to the binding; this will straighten and secure the finished piece.

HOW TO PREPARE THE FOUNDATION

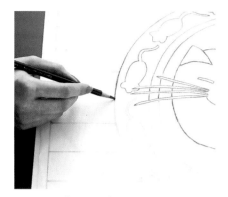

1 Trace design of rug in actual size on a lightweight sheet of paper, allowing for some background area around design motifs.

2 Cut the foundation fabric at least 8" (20.5 cm) larger than finished rug size; fold masking tape around raw edges to prevent raveling. Center finished rug size on foundation; mark, using a permanent-ink marking pen and following grainline of fabric.

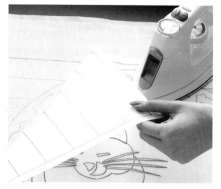

3 Trace the design onto back side of paper pattern, using a transfer pencil. Transfer design to foundation fabric, following the manufacturer's directions, making sure design is aligned with marked lines on the foundation.

4 Fold back ½" (1.3 cm) at end of prewashed twill tape. Stitch outer edge of twill tape to right side of the foundation fabric, with the outer edge positioned just inside marked lines and with folded end of tape at middle of one side; pivot at corners. Trim excess tape, overlapping ends ¾" (2 cm).

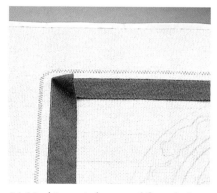

5 Machine-stitch around foundation fabric, using zigzag stitch, ½" (1.3 cm) outside previous stitching; at corners, stitch diagonally as shown. This machine stitching strengthens the finished rug.

6 Fold back twill tape; hand-baste to foundation. At corners, pull twill tape away from design area with stitches.

HOW TO PREPARE THE WOOL

1 Wash wool fabric in warm water with a mild detergent, washing it by hand or by machine in the gentle cycle; line dry or machine dry. Tear or cut wool into 9" × 12" (23 × 30.5 cm) pieces.

2 Cut several lengthwise strips, ¼" (6 mm) wide, from fabric pieces, taking care to follow grainline of fabric. Cut limited amounts as needed, as you hook the rug.

HOW TO HOOK A RUG

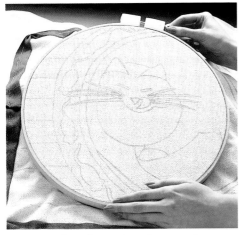

1 Secure foundation in a frame or hoop; fabric should be very taut.

2 Hold rug hook in palm of hand, above design, with hook turned up. Hold wool strip between thumb and forefinger of opposite hand; this hand will be held beneath the frame and will guide wool strip, making sure it does not twist.

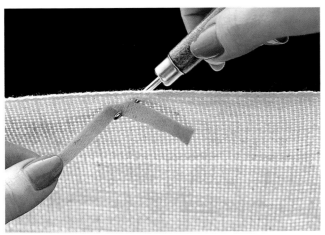

3 Push rug hook down through foundation, and catch the wool strip in hook. Pull end of wool strip to right side, to a height of about 1" (2.5 cm).

4 Continue hooking wool strip, skipping about two squares in foundation between each insertion of rug hook; pull wool loops to a height of about ¼" (6 mm). Evenly space loops, with no gaps between them, and do not twist wool strip.

5 Allow end of wool strip to extend above foundation on right side; reinsert rug hook in same opening to begin hooking second strip.

6 Clip ends of wool strips even with loops when each design area is completed, taking care not to clip loops.

HOW TO FINISH THE EDGES OF A HOOKED RUG

1 Remove hand basting from twill tape. Trim excess foundation fabric just beyond zigzag stitching.

2 Fold twill tape to underside of rug, mitering the corners; pin in place.

3 Hand-stitch twill tape in place, catching stitches in foundation fabric only. Stitch overlapped ends of tape together, and stitch along mitered corners.

4 Place the rug face down on a clean, flat ironing surface; cover with a dampened towel, and steam press. If shape of rug is distorted, gently straighten or ease it into shape. Allow rug to dry for 24 hours.

5 Make casing for wall hanging, if desired, by hand-stitching twill tape ¼" (6 mm) from upper and lower edges of rug. End the upper casing 1" (2.5 cm) from sides of rug.

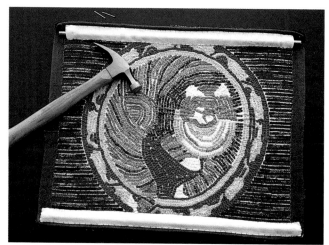

6 Insert a metal rod of ¼" or ⅜" (6 mm or 1 cm) diameter into each casing. Stitch ends of lower casing closed. Hang rug on wall by supporting rod on nails.

MORE
IDEAS FOR
HOOKED
RUGS

Traditional design *is hooked with a background of subtle color variation. When using a hooked rug on a hardwood or tile floor, place a thin rubber pad under the rug.*

Child's drawing, *enlarged on a photocopy machine, is used for the design of this pillow. Wool border strips, instead of the usual twill-tape binding, are stitched to the edges of the foundation fabric.*

Quilt design, *hooked in jewel-tone colors, is inspired by an Amish quilt.*

Use scraps of fabric to create rugs, placemats, chair seat mats, and trivets. Easy to make with a single crochet stitch, these rugs and mats can be either round or oval. They are so washable, they actually improve with age. Launder them by machine, and lay them flat to dry; for rugs, use a heavy-duty machine.

Use fabrics of 100 percent cotton or cotton blends in solid colors and patterns. For a rug or chair pad, use lightweight to mediumweight fabrics cut into strips 1⅜" (3.5 cm) wide. For a thinner placemat or trivet, use lightweight fabrics cut into 1" (2.5 cm) strips. For a 24" × 36" (61 × 91.5 cm) rug, you will need about 18 yd. (16.56 m) of 45" (115 cm) fabric; for a 13" (33 cm) chair pad, 2½ yd. (2.3 m); for a 12" × 18" (30.5 × 46 cm) placemat, 3¼ yd. (3.0 m); and for an 8" (20.5 cm) trivet, 1 yd. (0.95 m).

The strips are stitched together by machine, then folded and rolled into balls for easier handling during crocheting. For a variegated rug, alternate fabric strips in a single ball. For a more banded look, make a separate ball of each fabric.

To fold the strips quickly and easily, use a bias tape maker, available at fabric stores and from mail-order suppliers. The tape maker automatically folds the strip as you press it.

MATERIALS

FOR THICKER RUGS & CHAIR SEATS

- Lightweight or mediumweight fabric yardage or rags in cotton or cotton blends, cut into 1⅜" (3.5 cm) strips on crosswise or lengthwise grain.
- Size "J" crochet hook and ¾" (2 cm) bias tape maker.

FOR THINNER PLACEMATS & TRIVETS

- Lightweight fabric yardage or rags in cotton or cotton blends, cut into 1" (2.5 cm) strips on crosswise or lengthwise grain.
- Size "I" crochet hook and ½" (1.3 cm) bias tape maker.

Rag rugs and mats, *suitable for many uses, may be either round or oval. The rug and chair mat opposite are thicker than the placemats and the trivet above.*

HOW TO CROCHET A ROUND RAG RUG OR MAT

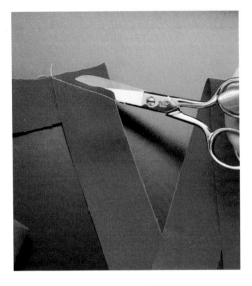

1 Place two strips of fabric, right sides together, at right angles to each other; stitch diagonally across the end, and trim ¼" (6 mm) from stitching. Repeat for several strips of same color or random colors.

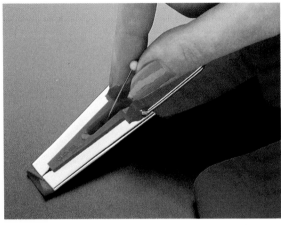

2 Thread fabric strip through channel at wide end of tape maker, bringing strip out at narrow end. Insert pin in slot opening to push strip through.

3 Pull fabric through tape maker, to fold raw edges to center of strip; press folds in place.

4 Press strip in half to make double-fold tape; roll into ball.

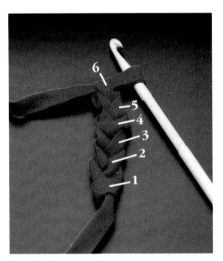

5 Crochet six chain stitches as on page 275, steps 1 to 5.

6 Join chain into a ring with a slip stitch by inserting hook into last chain stitch from hook; pass strip over hook.

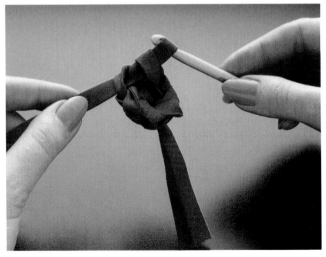

7 Draw strip through both chain and loop in one motion to complete slip stitch.

8 Crochet first round, working single crochet stitches as on page 275, steps 1 to 3; increase in all six stitches of the ring.

9 Stitch the second round, working single crochet stitches by continuing in a spiral and increasing in every other stitch. After the second round, increase as necessary to maintain the shape and flatness of the rug. Increase less often on subsequent rounds.

10 Change colors or add new fabric strips as in step 1, opposite; stitch by machine or by hand.

11 Check flatness of rug often by laying rug on flat surface. If the rug cups, you have not increased often enough; if rug ripples, you have increased too often. Steam-press rug, and remove as many stitches as necessary; then crochet area again to correct the problem.

12 Finish the rug, when the desired size is reached, by trimming the strip narrower, gradually decreasing the width of the strip to ⅜" (1 cm). Refold the strip.

13 End crocheting with a slip stitch by inserting hook into a stitch, with strip over hook; pull strip through stitch and loop in one motion. Cut strip, leaving 8" (20.5 cm) tail. Pull the tail through the loop to secure.

14 Weave end of strip in and out of last round, using crochet hook; repeat for tail at center of rug. Hand-stitch the ends in place, using a needle and hand-sewing thread.

HOW TO CROCHET AN OVAL RAG RUG

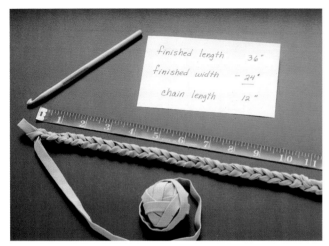

1 Subtract the desired finished width from the desired finished length; crochet a chain of stitches equal to this measurement, as in steps 1 to 5, opposite.

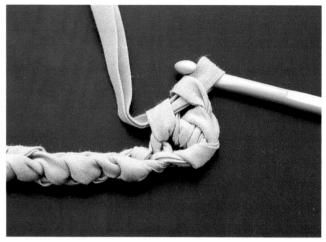

2 Work single crochet stitch in second stitch from hook, and increase, opposite.

3 Single crochet in each stitch of chain to end, without increasing. Single crochet four times in last stitch of chain to increase.

4 Single crochet in each stitch down opposite side of the chain, without increasing. At beginning end of chain, single crochet twice in same stitch as increased in step 2; this gives total of four single crochet stitches in that stitch.

5 Continue to stitch in spiraling rounds, single crocheting each stitch along straight sides; increase as necessary around curved ends to avoid cupping or rippling. Change colors and finish rug as on page 273, steps 10 to 14.

HOW TO MAKE CHAIN STITCHES

1 Starting. Grasp fabric strip about 2" (5 cm) from the end, between thumb and forefinger. With right hand, lap the long strand over the short one, forming a loop.

2 Hold loop in left hand. Grasp the crochet hook in right hand; insert crochet hook through loop, catching fabric strip.

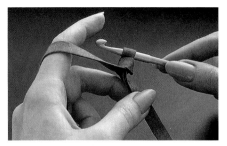

3 Draw strip through loop; pull loop tight. Lace the strip coming from ball through fingers of left hand and over index finger. Grasp bottom of the loop between thumb and middle finger.

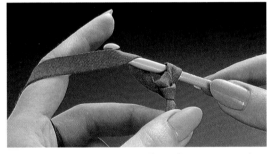

4 Chain stitch. Pass hook under strip. Catch strip with hook, and draw it through loop on hook. This makes one chain stitch.

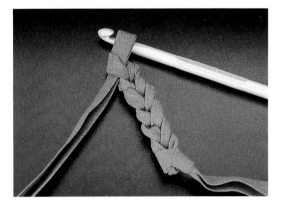

5 Repeat step 4 until chain reaches desired length or number of stitches. Loop on hook does not count as a stitch. If correct tension is used, chain stitches will be even in size.

HOW TO MAKE SINGLE CROCHET STITCHES

1 Insert the crochet hook under the top two strips from the previous row.

2 Wrap strip over hook, and draw it through chain only, leaving two loops on the hook.

3 Wrap strip over hook again; draw it through both loops on hook, completing one single crochet. When done, one loop is left on hook.

Increasing. Work two single crochets in the same stitch to increase.

275

PAINTED
FLOOR CLOTHS

Express your creativity by making a custom floor cloth with decorative painting or stenciling. Used at the entryway to the living room or as an area rug, a floor cloth can become an artwork conversation piece.

When designing the floor cloth, you may want to browse through art books or quilt books for design ideas and use a photocopy machine to enlarge the design to the desired size. Or duplicate a design used elsewhere in the room, such as a fabric or wallpaper design. For a perfect color match, have the paint colors for the floor cloth custom-mixed to match the fabric or wallpaper swatches.

An 18-ounce (500 gram) or #8 canvas provides a durable surface for floor cloths and lies flat on the floor. It is available in widths up to 5 feet (152.5 centimeters) at tent and awning stores and upholstery shops.

Paint the canvas, using latex paints intended for floors and patios. These paints are very durable and can be custom-mixed by the quart (0.9 liter). Or stencil the canvas, using oil-based paint crayons designed for stenciling; this type of paint will not bleed when applied to the fabric. To protect the floor cloth from abrasion, seal it with a nonyellowing latex urethane acrylic finish.

If the rug will be placed on a smooth floor surface, such as linoleum or ceramic, place a nonslip pad under the floor cloth.

HOW TO MAKE A PAINTED FLOOR CLOTH

MATERIALS

- 18-oz. (500 g) or #8 canvas.

- Latex floor paints in desired colors, paint roller, roller tray, and paintbrushes, for painted floor cloth.

- Oil-based paint crayons and stencil brushes, for stenciled floor cloth.

- Sealer, such as a nonyellowing latex urethane acrylic finish.

- Synthetic-bristle paintbrush, for applying sealer.

- Plastic drop cloth; carpenter's square; straightedge.

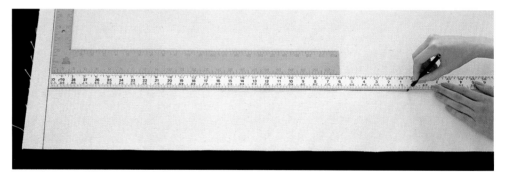

1 Trim selvages from canvas. Mark canvas to desired size, using pencil, carpenter's square, and straightedge; cut canvas.

2 Machine-stitch around the canvas ¼" (6 mm) from raw edges; stitch a second row of stitching ⅛" (3 mm) from raw edges. Press canvas so it lies flat.

3 Place canvas on a plastic drop cloth. Using paint roller, apply background color of paint, taking care not to crease canvas; roll paint in all directions to penetrate fabric. Allow to dry. Apply additional coats as necessary; allow to dry overnight. Trim any loose threads.

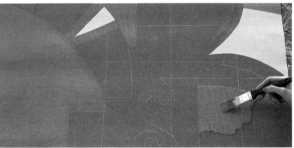

4 Mark design, if desired, using pencil. Paint desired design, applying one color at a time. Use a fine-pointed brush for outlining and wider brush for filling in design areas. Allow paint to dry 24 hours.

5 Apply sealer, using synthetic-bristle paintbrush; allow to dry several hours. Apply two additional coats of sealer, following manufacturer's instructions for drying time.

Stenciled floor cloth. Prepare the canvas as in steps 1 and 2, opposite. Stencil design. Apply sealer as in step 5, left.

Quilt design has been enlarged for this floor cloth.

Geometric fabric design was mimicked
to create a coordinating floor cloth.

Stenciled rug echoes the design applied to the walls.

Wreaths,
Garlands
& More

SALAL & BOXWOOD WREATHS

Wreaths beautifully accent doors and walls, whether decorated for a particular season or embellished to coordinate with the decorating scheme of a room. Long-lasting beauty can be achieved by using everlasting foliage for the base and dried or preserved flowers for embellishments. Fresh salal or boxwood is an ideal choice for the base. About a week after the wreath is made, the leaves dry and curl, resulting in a beautiful display of medium to pale green foliage. To preserve the wreath's beauty, hang it away from humidity and direct sunlight. The foliage can be secured to either a wire or straw base, in small bunches or one stem at a time, depending on the fullness of the stems.

HOW TO MAKE A WIRE-BASE SALAL WREATH

MATERIALS

- Fresh salal.
- Dried roses or other dominant flowers.
- Preserved statice or other filler flowers.
- Wire wreath base.
- 22-gauge or 24-gauge paddle floral wire, cut in lengths of 15" to 18" (38 to 46 cm).
- Wire cutter.
- Hot glue gun and glue sticks.

1 Cut fresh salal into lengths ranging from 6" to 8" (15 to 20.5 cm). Cluster four to six lengths together, and wrap with wire. Place cluster on the wire base; secure by wrapping wire from cluster around the base, crossing it in back, and twisting ends together in front.

2 Secure additional salal clusters to base, overlapping each to conceal wire, until entire base is covered.

3 Secure embellishments to wreath, using hot glue. Insert dominant flowers first, followed by filler flowers; space all embellishments evenly throughout wreath.

4 Hang wreath in desired location, and allow to dry. Rotate wreath occasionally while drying, so the leaves curl evenly around the wreath's natural curve.

HOW TO MAKE A STRAW-BASE SALAL WREATH

MATERIALS

- Ready-made straw wreath.
- Fresh salal; fresh seeded eucalyptus.
- Dried roses and cockscomb or other dried flowers.
- Dried bear grass.

- Sheet moss.
- Wire cutter; floral pins; floral tape.
- 3" (7.5 cm) floral picks with wire.
- Hot glue gun and glue sticks.

1 Secure sheet moss to the top and sides of straw wreath, using hot glue. Mist the sheet moss lightly before securing, if desired, to make it more pliable.

2 Cut fresh salal stems to within 2" to 3" (5 to 7.5 cm) of lower leaves, using wire cutter; secure several stems to wreath, using floral pins. Stagger salal, covering inside, top, and outside of wreath.

3 Continue covering wreath with salal, overlapping as necessary to conceal floral pins. It is not necessary to cover moss entirely, since it contributes to the design.

4 Cut dried flower stems to lengths ranging from 4" to 6" (10 to 15 cm); wire them to floral picks. Insert dried flowers into wreath as desired.

284

5 Insert seeded eucalyptus into wreath, securing with hot glue. Conceal ends of eucalyptus under salal, and weave branches through salal to hold them in place. Wire several stems of bear grass to floral picks, and insert into wreath as desired.

6 Hang wreath in desired location, and allow to dry. Rotate wreath occasionally while drying, so the leaves curl evenly around the wreath's natural curve.

HOW TO MAKE A WIRE-BASE OR STRAW-BASE BOXWOOD WREATH

1 Make wire-base wreath as on page 282, steps 1 and 2, or make straw-base wreath, opposite, steps 1 to 3; substitute fresh boxwood for salal. Attach embellishments such as pomegranates, roses, artichokes, pepper grass, and pepper berries to wreath, securing them with hot glue.

2 Hang wreath in desired location, and allow to dry. Rotate the wreath occasionally while drying, so leaves curl evenly around the wreath's natural curve.

Grapevine wreaths can complement any decorating style. Available at craft stores, grapevine bases come in a variety of sizes. Adding honeysuckle vine to the base can enlarge the size and create a loose, airy design with a woodsy look. A compact design can be made by covering parts of a grapevine wreath with sheet moss, creating a solid base for securing flower heads. Embellish the wreath with a wine bottle, clusters of grapes, and clay pots for the wine-country wreath shown here. Or choose from a variety of other embellishments to make the wreaths on pages 288 and 289.

MATERIALS

- Grapevine wreath.
- Honeysuckle vine.
- Dried hydrangeas and lavender.
- Mixed dried herbs.
- Silk ivy.
- Artificial grape clusters.

- Two clay pots.
- Empty wine bottle.
- Raffia.
- Wire cutter; 22-gauge paddle floral wire.
- Hot glue gun and glue sticks.

GRAPEVINE WREATHS

HOW TO MAKE A WINE-COUNTRY GRAPEVINE WREATH

1 Attach several strands of honeysuckle vine to wreath, securing with floral wire. Wrap vine loosely around wreath, allowing the strands to extend from the grapevine base; secure.

2 Apply hot glue to bottom of a wine bottle, and insert it into clay pot. Wrap floral wire below rim of pot, twisting to secure it; leave 5" (12.5 cm) ends. Glue wire to pot on two sides. Secure pot to wreath, using wire ends; glue pot to the wreath.

3 Tie raffia around pot to conceal wire and glue. Glue pieces of moss to wreath as desired.

4 Break remaining clay pot. Glue large pieces near base of pot with wine bottle; glue smaller pieces to wreath as desired.

5 Cut ivy apart; insert stems into wreath, securing with hot glue. Weave ivy around honeysuckle vines.

6 Insert grape clusters into wreath, securing with hot glue; concentrate clusters near wine bottle.

7 Apply hot glue to hydrangeas; secure to wreath. Bundle lavender, and place at bottom. Fill in bare areas with dried herbs; secure.

Heart wreath is embellished with sheet moss, potted roses, lavender bunches, and pepper berries.

Miniature wreaths are paired for impact. Sheet moss, pansies, and yellow rosebuds accent the wreaths for a romantic look.

Fruit wreath (opposite), wrapped with silver-dollar eucalyptus and artificial maple leaves, is covered with artificial fruit and dried fruit slices. Pinecones and sticks give the arrangement a woodsy look.

Autumn wreath has a grapevine base with added foliage. Fruits, vegetables, hydrangeas, poppy pods, and potted sunflowers embellish the wreath. Honeysuckle vine encircles the wreath.

A grapevine swag is easily made from a purchased grapevine wreath that has been cut in half. Hang a swag above a fireplace, or use it to decorate a wall.

Embellish the swag as desired to coordinate it with the surrounding decorating scheme. Flowers such as larkspur may replace the caspia, and a rose bundle may be substituted for the wheat sheaf.

MATERIALS

- Purchased grapevine wreath.
- Eucalyptus in two colors or other line materials.
- Dried canella berries or other desired berries.
- Dried caspia or other filler material.
- Dried wheat sheaf or other bundled material.
- 22-gauge or 24-gauge paddle floral wire; wire cutter.
- Hot glue gun and glue sticks.

HOW TO MAKE A GRAPEVINE SWAG

1 Cut the grapevine wreath in half, using a wire cutter or pruning shears. Join the halves as shown, securing them with wire.

2 Apply hot glue liberally to ends of eucalyptus, working with one color at a time; insert pieces around center of swag, spacing evenly and varying placement depth.

3 Apply glue to stems of canella berries, and insert into swag; intersperse berries among eucalyptus, varying placement depth.

4 Attach wheat sheaf to center of arrangement, applying glue generously to the sheaf and pressing it firmly into place. Hold for 5 minutes, to allow time for glue to set.

5 Apply glue to sprigs of caspia; insert into garland to fill in any bare areas as necessary.

FLEXIBLE GARLANDS

Garlands are versatile accessories for any room. They can be draped over headboards, shelves, pictures, or doorways. Flexible silk garlands are easily made by twisting wired flowers to an ivy garland. Nonwired materials can be attached to the garland, if desired, by securing them with floral wire.

HOW TO MAKE A FLEXIBLE GARLAND

MATERIALS

- Silk roses or other dominant flowers.
- Silk alstroemeria and astilbe or other secondary flowers.
- Silk miniature roses or other filler flowers.
- One 9-ft. (2.75 m) silk ivy garland.
- Two silk ivy plants, one solid green and one variegated.
- 22-gauge paddle floral wire and wire cutter, if silk flowers are not wired.

1 Cut stems from ivy plants; to add fullness, wrap the stems around garland, allowing some tendrils to extend.

2 Insert roses, spacing them evenly throughout the garland; secure by wrapping the stems around garland.

3 Insert astilbe into garland between roses, wrapping the stems around garland. Insert alstroemeria, spacing evenly; wrap the stems around garland.

4 Insert miniature roses to fill in any bare areas; wrap stems around garland.

SHAPED GARLANDS

Delicate-looking floral garlands add a romantic touch to walls or tables. For impact, drape a garland over a large mirror or shape one around a doorway to soften the straight lines and square corners. A shaped garland can also serve as a centerpiece when arranged down the center of a dining room table.

Create the base of the garland by encasing an evergreen garland in Spanish moss. For longer garlands, secure two or more evergreen garlands together.

MATERIALS

- One 6-ft. (1.85 m) evergreen garland.
- Silk hydrangeas and wild roses or other dominant flowers.
- Silk freesia or other secondary flowers.
- Silk baby's breath, astilbe, and wild berry sprays or other filler materials.
- Two 9-ft. (2.75 m) ivy garlands.

- Silk ivy plant.
- Berry vine.
- Spanish moss.
- Huckleberry twigs and honeysuckle vine, optional.
- Ribbon, optional.
- Fishing line.
- Wire cutter.
- Hot glue gun and glue sticks.

HOW TO MAKE A SHAPED GARLAND

1 Surround evergreen garland with Spanish moss, so the evergreen is barely visible; moss adheres to garland. Tie fishing line to garland at one end, and spiral it around the garland, encasing the moss; tie fishing line at opposite end. (White cord was used for clarity.)

2 Wrap ivy garlands around base in opposite directions, twisting vines around base to secure. Wrap berry vine around evergreen garland, allowing some tendrils to extend. Cut stems from ivy plant, and glue stems to garland, allowing some tendrils to extend.

3 Cut all flower stems to lengths ranging from 3" to 5" (7.5 to 12.5 cm). Secure hydrangeas and wild roses, one variety at a time, by applying hot glue to lower 1½" (3.8 cm) of stems.

4 Secure freesia to garland, as in step 3. Space the flowers evenly throughout the garland.

5 Apply glue to ends of the filler flowers, and insert them into the garland, one variety at a time, to fill in any bare areas. Insert twigs, vines, and ribbon, if desired.

295

HONEYSUCKLE GARLANDS

A decorative honeysuckle garland can adorn a table, wall, or mantel. Garlands can be filled with wisps of greenery or short, dense foliage, depending on the lengths of the floral materials used.

Garlands made of dried materials are fragile, and large garlands can be difficult to carry and arrange after they are finished. Therefore, you may want to construct the garland in the location where it will be displayed.

HOW TO MAKE A HONEYSUCKLE GARLAND

MATERIALS

- Honeysuckle vines.
- Preserved plumosa or other foliage.
- Silk and parchment roses or other dominant flowers.
- Dried pepper berries and nigella pods or other secondary materials.
- Dried pepper grass, statice, and veronica or other filler materials.
- Wire cutter.
- Paddle floral wire.
- Ribbon.

1 Cut the honeysuckle vines to arcs of desired lengths; secure together, using floral wire.

2 Insert sprigs of plumosa into vines until the desired fullness is achieved; secure with hot glue. Short stems make a more compact design.

3 Insert largest rose into center of garland to create a focal point. Insert remaining roses, spacing them evenly throughout garland; secure with hot glue.

4 Insert pepper berries so they radiate from central focal point; space evenly. Insert nigella pods, spacing evenly throughout.

5 Insert pepper grass, statice, and veronica, one variety at a time, radiating from the focal point. Insert ribbon into garland, forming loops at center; secure with hot glue.

TOPIARIES

Topiaries are unique floral arrangements that can be used alone or in pairs for a classic look on a fireplace mantel or buffet table. The base of a topiary can be a candlestick, as shown here. Or it can be a branch or a wooden dowel set into plaster of Paris. At the top, a cone or ball is covered with moss, vines, and other floral embellishments. The cone or ball may be either a Styrofoam® or grapevine form.

Candlestick topiaries are embellished with silk and dried floral materials for a romantic look.

Moss topiaries *are displayed as a pair. The topiary on the left has two twigs intertwined to form the trunk. The topiary on the right is a simple variation, with the moss-covered sphere glued directly to the rim of the pot.*

Floor topiary *is embellished with honeysuckle vine, dried greens, and dried floral materials.*

Fruit topiary *is decorated with fruit slices, artificial fruit, and ribbon.*

299

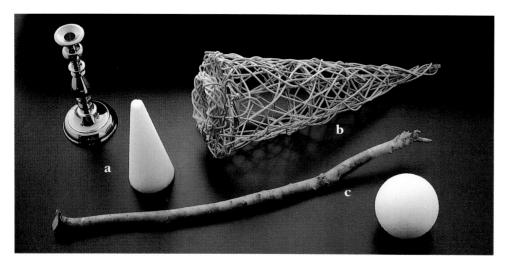

Topiaries can be made from a candlestick and a Styrofoam® cone **(a).** Or for a topiary set in plaster of Paris, you can use a branch and a grapevine cone **(b)** or Styrofoam ball **(c).**

HOW TO MAKE A TOPIARY WITH A CANDLESTICK BASE

MATERIALS

- Silk roses, hydrangeas, and wild roses or other dominant flowers.
- Silk rose hips and astilbe and dried lepidium or other filler flowers.
- Artificial berries; huckleberry or other twigs.

- Silk ivy or other leafy plant.
- Candlestick; Styrofoam cone.
- Spanish moss.
- Wire cutter; floral adhesive clay; floral pins.
- Hot glue gun and glue sticks.

1 Place a ring of floral adhesive clay around the outer rim of candlestick. Apply hot glue generously over top of candlestick; allow glue to cool slightly. Center the base of Styrofoam cone over the candlestick. Press cone down into glue and floral adhesive clay, twisting slightly to secure.

2 Cover the cone lightly with Spanish moss; secure with floral pins. Cut ivy stems from plant, using a wire cutter. Insert stems into foam; wrap ivy tightly around the cone, securing with floral pins. Insert the stems of berries into cone, spacing them evenly.

3 Cut rose stems to lengths of 2" (5 cm); insert into cone, one variety at a time, spacing them evenly. Insert the hydrangeas throughout topiary, spacing evenly. Extend the length of hydrangea stems, if necessary.

4 Cut lepidium, rose hips, and astilbe to lengths ranging from 3" to 6" (7.5 to 15 cm); insert evenly throughout topiary, one variety at a time. Bend stems, and shape flowers and leaves as necessary to balance arrangement and to cover any bare areas. Embellish with twigs.

HOW TO MAKE A TOPIARY WITH A PLASTER OF PARIS BASE

MATERIALS

- Floral materials, such as moss, artificial fruits, and dried naturals.
- Wooden box, ceramic pot, or other desired container.
- Grapevine or Styrofoam® cone or ball.
- Branch, twigs, or dowel for trunk.

- Plaster of Paris; disposable container for mixing.
- Heavy-duty aluminum foil.
- Saw, floral wire, and wire cutter may be needed for some projects, depending on floral materials selected.
- Hot glue gun and glue sticks.

1 Grapevine form. Line container with two layers of aluminum foil. Crumple foil loosely to shape of container, to allow room for plaster to expand as it dries; edge of foil should be about ¾" (2 cm) below top of container.

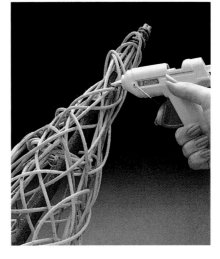

2 Insert trunk of tree into grapevine form as far as it will go. Place trunk in container, and adjust height of the topiary by cutting trunk to desired length. Secure grapevine form to trunk, using hot glue.

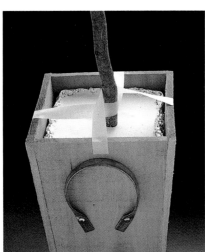

3 Mix the plaster of Paris, following manufacturer's instructions. Pour plaster into the container, filling to edge of foil. When plaster has started to thicken, insert trunk, making sure it stands straight. Support trunk, using tape as shown, until plaster has set.

4 Conceal plaster with moss or items that will be used to decorate topiary. Embellish grapevine form as desired.

Styrofoam form. Prepare container as in step 1, above. Insert trunk of topiary into foam ball or cone to one-half the diameter of ball. Place trunk in the container, and adjust the height of topiary by cutting trunk to desired length. Apply hot glue into hole in foam ball; place ball on trunk. Continue as in steps 3 and 4, above.

Floral
Accessories

DECORATIVE
CONTAINERS

A basket, box, or vase can be decorated with moss, leaves, or other floral materials to create a unique container for an arrangement. The base for the container may be made from a cardboard or wooden box, a glass vase, or a terra-cotta pot. The decorative containers may be embellished with a raffia or ribbon bow.

MATERIALS

- Basket, box, vase, or terra-cotta pot.
- Silk or preserved leaves, moss, pinecones, or flowers.
- Hot glue gun and glue sticks, or thick white craft glue.
- Raffia or ribbon, optional.

HOW TO MAKE DECORATIVE CONTAINERS

Leaves. Secure silk or preserved leaves in rows to vase or other container, using hot glue; overlap leaves as necessary to cover container. Leaves may be wrapped over the rim of the container, if desired. Embellish the container with raffia or ribbon as desired.

Pinecones. Cover cardboard box lightly with sheet moss; secure with hot glue. Cut the scales from one side of the pinecones, to make flat surface. Using hot glue, secure pinecones to sides of box with all pinecones facing in the same direction.

Moss. Secure sheet moss to sides of terra-cotta pot, using hot glue; cover the pot completely, and allow moss to extend slightly above the rim of the container.

Flowers. Secure flower petals to container, using thick white craft glue. For added embellishment, apply glue to the underside of flower heads and leaves; secure to the sides of the container.

DECORATING WIRE FORMS

Wire forms in various shapes and sizes can be covered with sheet moss for the look of a professionally groomed garden topiary. The forms, available from garden centers, craft stores, and mail-order suppliers, are first wrapped with wire mesh, then with the sheet moss, as shown below.

Other wire forms, such as bird cages, can be embellished with ivy vines, flowers, berries, and ribbons, using your creativity. Simply twist the vines around the wire forms, and use a hot glue gun to secure other embellishments.

HOW TO DECORATE WIRE FORMS

MATERIALS

- Wire form in desired shape, such as animal form.
- Wire mesh, such as chicken wire.
- Sheet moss.
- Wire cutter; paddle floral wire.

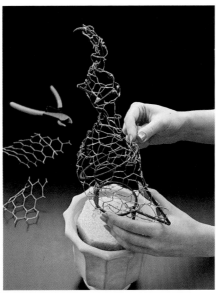 

1 Place wire mesh over wire form, folding it around wire contours. Clip away any excess mesh, using a wire cutter; wrap wire ends around form as necessary to secure.

2 Mist the sheet moss lightly with water to make it more pliable. Cover wire form with sheet moss, securing it with floral wire.

Wire forms *can be covered with sheet moss, as shown on the animal forms. Or accent wire forms like the bird cage and sphere topiary with vines, flowers, and foliage.*

POMANDERS

Pomanders made from fragrant floral materials add a delicate aroma to a room. Hang pomanders decoratively in the center of a window or doorway. Or group them together to fill a bowl or basket, perhaps for a centerpiece on the dining-room table.

Fruit pomanders are created by shaping foam eggs and balls to resemble fruit shapes. Decorate them with flowers, petals, and leaves.

Pomander is covered with rose petals. Rosebuds, plumosa, and ribbons, secured with hot glue, add a finishing touch to the top of the pomander. The pomander may be tied to a lamp pull or bedpost.

Leaf-covered spheres are decorated with leaves. The leaves may be secured with glue, or secure them with brads for a decorative accent. Combine spheres of different sizes and types, grouping them together in a basket.

HOW TO MAKE FRUIT POMANDERS

MATERIALS

- Lavender, boxwood leaves, yarrow, rose petals, sunflower petals, globe amaranth, marigold petals or other desired floral materials.
- Dried or silk leaves, such as lemon verbena, pineapple, and grape.
- Twigs; cloves.
- Styrofoam® balls, eggs, and wreaths of various sizes, depending on the kinds and sizes of fruit desired.
- Wire cutter; serrated knife.
- Low-temperature glue gun and glue sticks; thick white craft glue.

1 Grapes. Apply white glue to small foam balls; roll the balls in lavender blossoms to cover. Allow to dry.

2 Form a grape cluster by securing several lavender-covered balls to 3" to 4" (7.5 to 10 cm) twig, using glue gun. Secure silk or dried leaf to end.

1 Pear. Press end of foam egg against table; roll gently from side to side to form shape for end of pear. Smooth the shape by pressing foam with fingers as necessary.

2 Apply white glue to foam; roll pear in boxwood leaves or yarrow to cover. Insert 2" (5 cm) twig into end of pear; secure, using glue gun.

1 Apple. Press a foam ball against table; roll lower two-thirds of ball gently from side to side to flatten and narrow slightly for bottom of apple.

2 Insert knife into top of apple at an angle; cut out a small cone shape about ½" (1.3 cm) long. Repeat at bottom of apple, cutting out a cone shape about ¼" (6 mm) long.

3 Smooth sharp edges by pressing foam with fingers. Apply white glue to foam, and roll in rose petals to cover. Insert 2" (5 cm) twig and lemon verbena leaves into top of apple; secure, using glue gun.

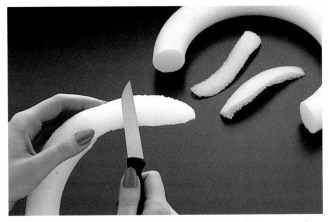

1 Banana. Cut 10" (25.5 cm) arc from Styrofoam wreath form; shape banana by trimming ends to points.

2 Apply white glue to foam; roll in sunflower petals to cover. Insert cloves into ends.

Pineapple. Trim lower end of foam egg to form flat base. Glue a stick into bottom of egg to make decorating easier. Apply glue to globe amaranth, using glue gun; insert pineapple leaves into top, securing with glue gun. Trim stick from base.

Orange. Make indentation in top and bottom of foam ball, using finger. Apply white glue to foam; roll in marigold petals to cover. Insert clove at each end.

HOW TO MAKE LEAF-COVERED POMANDERS

MATERIALS

- Styrofoam balls.
- Preserved, artificial, or fresh leaves.
- Low-temperature glue gun and glue sticks, or decorative brads.

Spheres with leaves. Secure leaves in rows to foam balls, using glue; each row overlaps leaves of previous row.

Spheres with leaves and brads. Secure leaves in rows to foam balls, inserting decorative brad at tip of each leaf to secure; each row overlaps leaves of previous row.

FLORAL BUNDLES

Long-stemmed dried naturals bundled in decorative containers make simple, attractive arrangements. Several bundles of various heights can be grouped for added impact.

For tall floral bundles, select a container that is heavy enough to support the height of the plant. If necessary, weight the bottom of the container with rocks or sand.

HOW TO MAKE A FLORAL BUNDLE

MATERIALS

- Dried naturals, such as roses, lavender, or rye.
- Decorative container.
- Floral arranging foam, such as by The John Henry Company.
- Sheet moss or Spanish moss; floral pins.
- 1½ yd. (1.4 m) ribbon or paper twist, optional.

1 Cut floral foam, using knife, so foam fits container snugly and is about ½" (1.3 cm) from top; cut and insert foam wedges as necessary. Cover foam with moss, securing it with floral pins.

2 Insert stems of dried naturals into foam, starting in center and working out in a circle until desired fullness is achieved. Stems in the outer rows may be shorter than in the center.

3 Wrap a ribbon or paper twist around the bundle, if desired; tie in a bow.

Tiered bundle of dried naturals
(above) is arranged in an oval
container. The bay leaves and
pomegranates at the base of the
stems add a finishing touch.

Wheat bundle (left) is arranged
in the usual manner, then tied
tightly and twisted to give it a
new shape. Dried hydrangeas
are clustered above the basket.

MORE IDEAS FOR FLORAL BUNDLES

Bundle of grain and flowers is arranged in a small, aged terra cotta pot. The bow is tied close to the pot, allowing the grain to flare gently.

Tiers of roses and cockscomb are simply arranged in a decorative pot.

Tiny dried roses are arranged in a small metal pot.

DRIED CORNUCOPIA CENTERPIECES

For an autumn feast, a cornucopia overflowing with dried naturals is a classic centerpiece. From the dozens of dried varieties available, select several, in a range of colors, shapes, and textures.

For a unique arrangement, consider using preserved roses, wheat, nigella pods, and yarrow instead of the more traditional gourds and Indian corn. For even more contrast in texture, accent the dried naturals with latex fruits.

To assemble the arrangement, fill the cornucopia with floral foam covered with moss. Then insert the dried naturals into the foam, one layer at a time.

MATERIALS

- Wicker cornucopia.
- Floral foam for dried arranging; sheet moss.
- Preserved autumn leaves; dried naturals, such as preserved roses, wheat, nigella pods, and yarrow.
- Latex or other artificial fruit, such as apples, grapes, and berries.
- 20-gauge floral wire; U-shaped floral pins; wired floral picks; hot glue gun and glue sticks.

HOW TO MAKE A DRIED CORNUCOPIA CENTERPIECE

1 Cut a piece of floral foam to fit inside cornucopia, using serrated knife. Insert wire through bottom of basket, then through foam.

2 Place a small piece of folded paper or cardboard on top of the foam, between wire ends; twist wire ends tightly over paper. This prevents wire from tearing the foam.

3 Cover foam loosely with moss; pin in place as necessary, using floral pins.

4 Insert the stems of the preserved leaves into the foam so leaves rest on table. Insert bunch of one type of dried naturals, such as nigella pods, into foam next to the leaves.

5 Insert cluster of latex grapes or other fruit on one side of the arrangement, above leaves. Wrap the wire from a floral pick around several stems of wheat; insert the pick into the foam near the center of arrangement, above leaves.

6 Insert several stems of roses in a cluster, next to grapes. Insert clusters of each remaining material, such as yarrow, arranging one variety at a time.

7 Fill in any bare areas with additional leaves or small grape clusters. Use hot glue, if necessary, to secure any individual items, such as single leaves, that cannot be inserted into foam.

INDEX

Stool covers, ruffled, 247-249
Swags, grapevine, 290-291

Cy DeCosse Incorporated offers
a variety of how-to books. For
information write:
  Cy DeCosse Subscriber Books
  5900 Green Oak Drive
  Minnetonka, MN 55343